THE *Silent* SON

THE
Silent
SON

What a Mentally Handicapped Child
Taught His Struggling Father About
LIFE, LOVE AND GOD

KEN ATKINS

NASHVILLE

NEW YORK • LONDON • MELBOURNE • VANCOUVER

THE *Silent* SON
What a Mentally Handicapped Child Taught His
Struggling Father About LIFE, LOVE AND GOD

Published in New York, New York, by Morgan James Publishing. Morgan James is a trademark of Morgan James, LLC. www.MorganJamesPublishing.com

All Biblical quotations from *The Holy Bible, New International Version, Zondervan*

ISBN 978-1-63195-064-3 paperback
ISBN 978-1-63195-065-0 eBook
Library of Congress Control Number: 2020903292

Cover Photo by:
Jacob Fryer

Cover Design by:
Rachel Lopez
www.r2cdesign.com

Morgan James is a proud partner of Habitat for Humanity Peninsula and Greater Williamsburg. Partners in building since 2006.

Get involved today! Visit
www.MorganJamesBuilds.com

TABLE OF CONTENTS

FOREWORD

The lives of our precious children are under siege. Statistics may vary slightly, depending on the source, but the message is the same: the incidence of childhood disability is drastically on the rise. If your life hasn't been impacted by this sad trend, it most likely will be at some point.

How do you cope, find encouragement and persevere under the greatest of challenges?

Being a pediatric physical therapist for 38 years, having a son born with an amputation of his left hand, and a great nephew who is in a wheelchair following a severe brain injury, I have experienced this world up close and personal. I have seen firsthand the struggles and the blessings of raising a child with special needs. I have witnessed my own son become a concert pianist with only one hand. I have seen a child whose parents were told he would never walk, take his first steps at the age of 7, to a room full of joyful tears. I have seen babies born with no connection between the hemispheres of the brain develop completely normally and live full, college bound lives. However, I have also cried with families grieving the loss of their child or mourning the loss of what could have and should have been.

Is this road easy? No. Is it rewarding? My experience says resoundingly, YES!

When Ken asked me to read an account of his journey, I was honored. Little did I realize how deeply it would impact me. Ken so masterfully takes us through the patchwork of heartaches and weaves a tapestry of triumph. It is a testimony to the indomitable spirit that lies within us all. No matter our struggle or our circumstances, always remember … But God!

The Silent Son is an amazingly honest window into the "beautifully messy" world of parenting a child with special needs. Ken's experiences, meshed with his wit and wisdom, make this a read that is hard to put down. The heartache and the joy are palpable. I found myself crying one minute and laughing the next, which I believe to be a true reflection of the journey.

In the book, Ken states, "I never cease to be amazed at how God uses people from our past to answer our prayers, bringing them back into our lives at the moment when we have given up hope." Similarly, I met Ken years ago, as a student in his early teaching days. Ironically (but God), our paths crossed again years later, as I became his son Danny's physical therapist for a season. Now, years later, we find ourselves together again, to celebrate the goodness of God.

I implore all parents, all professionals, and literally all people to read this book. You will be encouraged, educated, and experience true eucharistia (thanksgiving). Ken, thank you. God is honored, as are "the least of these."

Sheri Huling, PT

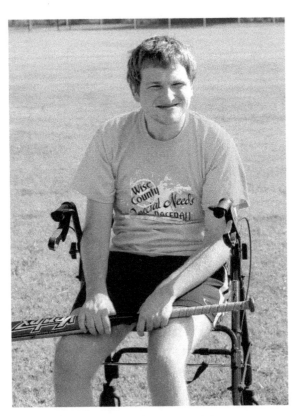

Danny Atkins at age 25

Introduction
A SIMPLE LIFE

"The plan was to get my degree, land a good teaching job, settle down in my small town, find a nice girl to marry, maybe have a kid or two, and spend my life surrounded by good friends. You know, just a quiet life and the simple, easy things like a cold beer and cooking steaks on the grill every Saturday."

The half dozen guys in my recovery support group stared into their coffee cups or laps and chuckled. The plans we all made seemed so clear and doable when we were teenagers. But years of bad choices, addictions, broken promises or unforeseen tragedies had left their scars, and here we were gathering once a week to admit that our lives had become unmanageable and we were powerless to fix them.

The stories were as varied as our backgrounds, but there was a common thread. None of us ever planned for it to turn out like this, and even though we couldn't change the past, we believed that, with God's help and our obedience, the future didn't have to be more of the same old, same old.

The one part of my life that set me apart from the rest, besides the fact that I was the only white dude in the group and at least twenty years older than most of the other guys, was that my adult son was sitting next to me in the meeting. Usually, our program doesn't allow family members in the same share group, because their presence can inhibit the openness and brutal honesty that is required to come to grips with the darkest parts of our broken psyches.

But it was OK because my son has been an ever-present appendage for my life almost since he was born, and certainly for the past eighteen years. Danny is twenty-seven. That's his chronological age. But in reality he will forever be eighteen months old. Danny has a genetic defect known as Angelman Syndrome, which manifests as severe mental retardation, and a very happy, almost always smiling, countenance. Shortly after his ninth birthday, his mother and I separated, and since that time I have been his primary caretaker and decision maker.

He has been by my side, literally, through divorces, a couple of major relocations, career changes, years of ever-deepening depression, alcoholism and now recovery. He has sat in the front seat of my truck patiently watching as I parked on the side of the road weeping uncontrollably, or lost my cool and yelled into the phone at significant others, or worked for hours in the blistering heat or freezing cold at one of the job sites where I earned my pay, or mindlessly put thousands of freeway miles on my truck taking him back and forth to spend time with his mother.

I realized a long time ago that this fact—having a handicapped child and now adult to care for—puts me in a unique and often overlooked part of society. We are admired, or pitied, or put on a pedestal, or complained about, or simply ignored, because we are different from most, and "most" don't know how to deal with us, so they just avoid us for fear that they might do or say the wrong thing.

Those of us in recovery often joke that we are "those people"—the ones that many churches have turned their backs on and really don't want to see or talk about, because of the bad choices we have made and the damage we have inflicted on ourselves and those around us. In short, good people avoid "those people" because "they" have problems that "good people" prefer to keep out of their lives.

It is basically the same for those in the handicapped world. I don't think most people have a dislike for us over here, they just don't know what to do with us. So best to just smile, nod and move on about their regular lives. Lord knows, every life has enough stress in it, handicap or no handicap.

Raising a child with special needs requires many special talents, special sacrifices and special strengths that you probably never realized you had before. But in more than a quarter century of dealing with all these challenges, what I have found is that the really "special" part of all this is the relationship you will have with the "special" child, and with all the significant others in your life—spouse, other children, dear friends, doctors, therapists, teachers and a handful of angels you will encounter along the way. And with your creator.

Danny is a strapping, healthy twenty-seven-year-old man with a mind that will be forever stuck in the pre-verbalite era. He loves people, and people love him. And though he will never speak a word, he has profoundly changed the lives of many, many people, starting with me.

This is his story—our story. And at the end perhaps you will see the many lessons I learned along the way. His story is not a tragedy, nor a heroic tale. It is the story God wrote for him, and it is pretty much the same one God writes for all of us. We just need to take a step back and try to look past our own selfish desires, fears and doubts.

This wasn't part of my life plan when I was getting out of high school. It wasn't part of my plan even when, at age forty, I welcomed him, my first child, into the world.

But it is what it is. And it is pretty darn amazing.

Chapter 1
THE RELUCTANT PARENT

*"For I know the plans I have for you," declares the Lord, "plans to
prosper you and not harm you, plans to give you hope and a future."*
– Jeremiah 29:11

I t is a typical Sunday afternoon. My twenty-six-year-old son is
on his twin bed, bent double, with feet on the floor, butt on
the edge of the bed and head resting on my office chair, having
spent several minutes getting perfectly placed in this very uncomfortable
looking resting position. He is paying no attention to the *SpongeBob*
rerun playing on his large screen TV. Oblivious to the world around
him, he quietly rubs his thumb back and forth over his mouth, an

activity that can occupy hours if left uninterrupted by me or our black cat who wanders in and out looking for someone to hit up for a quick game of swat or a back and head rub.

I am on my twin bed next to his, working the Sunday crossword, both glad for and resigned to the fact that this peace and quiet will last the entire afternoon, as long as I stay in the room with him, even though he seems to be totally unaware of my presence. Experience has taught me that if I leave the room for more than two minutes, he will be banging on the wall, demanding my return, so that he can resume his thumb-licking.

Such is the life of caring for a mentally handicapped person. It can be daunting, physically and emotionally challenging, scary, exhilarating, exhausting, even soul crushing. Mostly it can be incredibly monotonous.

But don't get me wrong. Raising my son has been the greatest joy and blessing I have ever known. It has taught me to be more patient, less self-centered, more organized, yet less structured. Mostly, it has taught me I can do many, many things I never imagined, but only by the grace and mercy of God.

I write this book as a message of hope and understanding for those who find themselves in this position with no idea what it means. There are no classes or instruction manuals for quick reference. There are lots of ideas, stories and suggestions that you will receive from family, friends, doctors, therapists and unlimited Internet sites. Some of it might even be helpful, but none of it should be accepted without careful examination.

Three things you should know before we start:

1. There is no single *right* way for raising your handicapped child. Every disability comes with a wide range of effects and effective treatments. Not all Downs kids are the same. Or CP kids. Or, in my son's case, AS (Angelman Syndrome) kids. Just like normal kids, special needs kids have a million subtle and

not-so-subtle differences between them and their peers with the same diagnosis. One of those differences, possibly the most important one, is you. How you adjust to this new life will have a huge impact on your beloved child (or adult). Which leads us to:

2. You will never totally get this the way you hope. There will be mistakes, tears, fears and moments of doubt and depression. Your old life is basically over, but that's not necessarily a bad thing. You will find yourself thinking more intentionally about what you can do to enhance your child's life, which may include getting rid of a lot of old, bad habits and distractions that needed dealt with anyway. One of the greatest gifts of this quarter century of raising my son has been that it forced me to do some serious soul searching and make some huge changes in how I live my life. With Angelman Syndrome, intellectual development pretty much stops at about eighteen months, so some things never change. Other than physical growth, Danny isn't much different than he has been his whole life, but I am a completely different—and better—person. And that leads me to:

3. I can't speak for anyone else, but I could not have done this without a deep faith in and dependence on God. If you find that idea foolish, then I suggest you return this book and get your refund now. Because without God, I would not be writing this; I'm not sure I would even be alive. One of the greatest results of this amazing journey so far has been realizing that God not only has a plan for Danny's disability, but that a significant part of that plan is to lead his dad back to his own heavenly father. My own depression, low self-esteem, relationship addiction and alcohol abuse were as important to God as Danny's mental and physical limitations. Thanks to

God, working through my nonverbal son, I finally found the strength to face my life-long demons.

So here is the story of a mentally challenged young man and his equally imperfect old man, and their journey through strange and wonderful waters.

■————————■

I never planned on being a father. Having already been through a couple of failed marriages and approaching my fortieth birthday, the dream of parenthood had long faded. Besides, I was too busy trying to make a name for myself as a writer and marketing professional to worry about kids.

Discovering that I was about to become a dad brought a crazy mixture of uncertainty, doubt, fear, dread and all those other wonderful things expectant parents feel. But as the big day approached, I began to warm to the idea.

Very early in the morning on the first day of spring in 1992, my wife and I were suddenly jolted out of our slumber by something which we both felt but at first couldn't pinpoint. We immediately sat up in bed and looked at each other confused and a bit fearful. I thought I had heard a pop somewhere, and my wife had felt something strange. It only took a few seconds for the sleep to clear and the reality to set in that her water had broken (about a week ahead of schedule), and off we rushed down blessedly traffic-free Dallas freeways to the hospital.

Thanks to some good financial decisions my wife had made prior to our marriage, we were able to afford what our ob-gyn referred to as the "North Dallas delivery." That meant a beautiful delivery suite, highly trained and attentive nurses, and an epidural applied early enough that the only way we knew my wife was having contractions was by watching the monitor.

The delivery was totally uneventful, which was perfect for me as I was an absolute bundle of sleep-deprived, over-caffeinated jitters. Possibly the happiest moment in my life came around noon that day when the doctor placed Danny in my arms. He was a healthy, happy baby whose fine blonde hair gave him almost an angelic appearance (I'm pretty sure I'm not the first person to think that about their newborn child).

In the beginning, life was beyond good. It was amazing. And exhausting. And frustrating. Danny was unable to nurse properly, which meant his mom had to spend lots of time pumping, and I had the opportunity to fully participate in the 2:00 a.m. feedings. His digestion was poor, leading to lots of crying, colic and long, late-night drives to soothe the beast.

But this new normal was just fine with us. We traded our copy of *What to Expect When You're Expecting* for a copy of *What to Expect: The First Year* and steeled ourselves for the bumpy ride ahead.

We waited anxiously for him to do all those precious things babies do—like learning to crawl, then stand, then walk, and utter those first babbling words. But nothing ever seemed to change. At the six-month checkup, our pediatrician lectured us for raising a tyrant since he wasn't eating any solid food yet, and demanded that we take control of the situation immediately. We did—we found a new, less condescending pediatrician.

Despite the underlying worries, life during that time was wonderful. Danny was happy, always smiling, laughing and waving his arms. He had an aura about him that just made him glow. He wasn't difficult, fitting easily into our small home-based publishing and marketing business. I took him to business meetings, church leadership training sessions, occasionally even to my weekly Rotary Club meetings. I was a proud father and he was the perfect companion.

One of my favorite memories (and this happened on several occasions) was being in a supermarket or Walmart and having some lady come over and stare at Danny in his car seat in awe. "What an absolutely beautiful baby," she would exclaim. Then she would look at me and gush, "He looks just like you!" Yes, good times indeed.

At the nine-month checkup, Danny's new doctor said she wasn't sure if he was just a late bloomer or there was something more serious going on, and suggested we visit a children's hospital in Dallas to do some preliminary genetic testing. The real answer would be much clearer by the twelve-month checkup, she said. And so we waited, and watched.

Danny's first birthday was a bittersweet celebration of the joy of the first year of his life, and the nagging worries about his lack of development. It was also the beginning of a life-changing journey that would take us far and wide, and run through tens of thousands of dollars in medical bills. The genetic testing ruled many possibilities out, but never gave us the definitive name for what we were facing. That was maddening, because without a name, we couldn't begin to focus our search for the right medicine or operation or therapy that would fix things. And that was our ultimate goal—to *fix* this *problem* and make Danny **normal.**

The summer of 1993 brought two big changes: our daughter Chrissy was born, and one of the members of our church life group introduced us to a Pennsylvania-based program for brain-injured children—the Institutes for the Achievement of Human Potential.

My wife's pregnancy with Chrissy had been somewhat difficult, particularly in the final weeks, but the delivery went just fine and we brought home another healthy, beautiful baby. Less than three months later, the four of us packed into our van and headed to Philadelphia to go through an intense, week-long session on fixing our brain-injured child.

On the second day of our trip, we finally got the call from the doctor giving us the answer we had been seeking. The latest genetic testing had confirmed that Danny's condition was known as Angelman Syndrome, a deletion in the fifteenth chromosome on the maternal side.

We had questioned our pediatrician about the possibility of Danny being an Angelman child after his grandmother had seen an article in a Florida newspaper about a professional baseball player whose daughter had Angelman Syndrome. We were struck by how much this little girl looked like our son and how many of her symptoms mirrored Danny's.

"Oh no," the doctor assured us. "I've been around Angelman kids and they are much more involved than he is. That's a pretty dire prognosis, and I think he is much more high-functioning."

"Involved." That's a key word in the special needs world. Let's just say that while a high degree of involvement is a good thing in a normal child's life, the opposite is true over here on the handicapped side of the fence. Being highly *involved* means that your child's condition affects a large number of basic life functions, such as walking, speech, continence, self-care and self-control.

Put another way, if you have a highly involved child to care for, you are going to be highly involved in meeting his or her most basic needs for as long as you can provide that care. Then you get to pass that responsibility on to someone else.

One of the things I love most about God is that He is faithful to dish out the bad news in manageable doses. I know our physician felt terrible about calling us over the Thanksgiving holiday to deliver the devastating news that Danny's condition was severe and lifelong, with little hope of a cure. But it couldn't have come at a better time. We were riding high all the way to Philadelphia with the promise of better, miraculous days ahead. The Institutes had done amazing things in the past with people much more involved than Danny. We believed that God had opened this door, and nothing could staunch our excitement.

Fortunately, this all occurred before the widespread use of the Internet and Wikipedia. Had we been able to read more about this expensive program, we might have had some doubts and possibly chosen not to give it a try.

Maybe. But we were pretty desperate. By this time, Danny was twenty months old and could not crawl, pull up, roll over, or even get up on all-fours. He made his noises, but nothing approaching words or even meaningful sounds.

Then, and now, the medical community took a fairly dim view of the Institutes' approach to treating brain injuries and lack of development through a rigid program of repetitious activities designed to increase the brain's functions. "We only use about 10 percent of our brain," they kept telling us again and again. We can't fix those parts that were damaged by an injury or just never developed, but we can stimulate other areas of the brain to take over those functions.

The training was intense, stimulating and exhausting—ten hours a day for a week. All these years later, I remember some of it. But mostly I remember the sweet, sad families from all over the world who were there to "fix" their imperfect kids. There was the middle-aged dad from Austin, Texas, whose daughter's perfect life as cheerleader, college student, gymnast and beautiful person came to an abrupt end at the hands of a drunk driver. Now she lay paralyzed and non-communicative. "I'm going to bring her back," he told me over afternoon coffee. "I know she'll never be what she was, but I'm going to bring her back to me."

There was the Hasidic Jewish couple from Israel—dad with his long beard and ringlet hair, mom with a newborn tucked under her shawl. They had come in hopes of fixing their Down's Syndrome son. We became brief but fast friends as our van provided a private place for her to nurse her baby.

This was my first encounter with a group of special needs family sojourners. I was touched by their hope and dedication. I was moved by their stories. And, in truth, I found myself giving quiet thanks that I didn't have their "problem" to face.

At the end of the week, the Institutes gave us a program to carry out when we returned home, taught us how to do the different tasks, sold us several hundred dollars' worth of equipment and books, made us sign an agreement that we would diligently and honestly follow the prescribed program, and sent us on our way. In the parking lot, the emotions of the week and the enormity of the challenge ahead finally hit me. I cried uncontrollably for nearly an hour. They were the first tears I had shed since Danny was born.

As part of the program prescribed by the Institutes, a bag filled with aluminum cans was strapped to Danny's lower back to keep him from rolling over on his bag while he learned to crawl. Within months, Danny was crawling a mile a day.

Chapter 2
THE PROGRAM

"When times are good, be happy; but when times are bad, consider:
God has made the one as well as the other."
— Ecclesiastes 7:14

I grew up on a small dairy farm, so I understood work and commitment. Neither of my parents worked off the farm. Our whole financial and social lives revolved around the daily needs of cows and crops.

I couldn't wait to get off the farm and get out into the *real* world. It's not that I didn't enjoy farm life. I just wanted to do something that didn't involve cow manure, drought, ornery bulls and the life-sucking monotony of milking twice a day seven days a week come hell, high water, death or Friday night football.

Little did I realize that it was precisely that training in a life of monotonous dedication and responsibility that would prepare me for my life starting at age forty. Many people experience this reality when they become parents of a newborn. The old habits and routines give way to new "child centered" activities, like diapering, non-stop laundry, soothing crying babies, cooing over sweet babies and showing said babies off to family and friends.

Often, old friendships fall by the wayside, as our running buddies have a hard time grasping why we are either unavailable or too tired to do anything. But we find ourselves making new friends at Mother's Day Out or church events for young families or chance encounters in the pediatrician's waiting rooms.

But old friends and dreams pale in comparison to the sweet joy of watching your child grow up right before your eyes.

Except when they don't.

At some point between eighteen and twenty-four months, a child should have already started walking and running, and possibly going up and down stairs unassisted. He should be scribbling with a pencil and creating structures with blocks. He should be feeding himself, using a spoon and fork. He should be showing signs of being ready for toilet training. One to seven words a week should start being added to the child's vocabulary, particularly descriptive words and phrases for the things around them, like clothes, toys and animal sounds. By the child's second birthday, he should know at least fifty words and be able to use them in two-word statements.

This wasn't just theoretical for us; it was in our faces everywhere we went. At the time, we were part of a church that seemed to be filled with young, fruitful couples. There were infants and toddlers everywhere, and they were all developing at normal rates, doing all the things they were supposed to be doing when they were supposed to be doing them.

Except Danny. When we started the program in earnest, Danny was twenty-one months old and he could not crawl, roll over or even hold himself up on all-fours. He had no speech and his receptive language was highly questionable. He couldn't use any feeding utensils, and finger foods were as likely to be flung across the room as they were to end up in his mouth. In fact, everything in the house ended up in his mouth, as he seemed obsessed about tasting whatever he picked up.

Each passing month brought more worry and, I am sorry to admit, embarrassment for us, as we continued to physically carry and spoon-feed our growing toddler who didn't toddle. Questions and concerns began to come from friends and family. They were sincere and well-intentioned, I am sure, but they were painful to face and difficult to answer.

That's where the isolation and loneliness can begin for parents of a handicapped child. Your old friends don't stop loving you. They just have no frame of reference to relate to your current crisis. And the new young-parent friends you have made disappear because they can't handle your heartbreak and fears, lest those emotions spill over into their highly stressed family lives. It's not that they don't care or share your pain; they just can't deal with it, and they feel guilty about that (as well as the guilt of having healthy, normal kids).

That was the world that my wife and I found ourselves in when we returned from Philadelphia with our kids, and Danny's program, in tow. In the beginning, we were showered with love and help from our church family, old friends and our actual families. Everyone offered something, from cooking meals to prayers to cash to just being there when we needed a break.

We quickly put together a team to help with the fourteen-hour-a-day program. Most of it could be done by either my wife or me (mostly my wife, as I tried to maintain some semblance of our marketing business). The mantra for the Institutes' program was "frequency, intensity and duration." It involved performing a routine of sensory stimulation, breathing exercises and a full-bodied assisted exercise known as "patterning."

Danny's brain wasn't physically damaged, it was just not functioning properly. The Institutes had shown us a video of a young man who had been severely injured in an accident, resulting in one half of his brain being removed. The brain has several divisions performing specific duties within the body—from controlling what you see and hear to regulating your breathing and body temperature. Through the Institutes' program, the remaining part of this man's brain had developed the necessary pathways to take over those functions that had been controlled by the missing part of his brain.

The brain is an incredibly complex and amazing organ, and there are many stories of damaged brains doing unbelievable things. It is always changing; in fact, recent research has shown that you can change the physical make-up of your brain through how you think. It is ever adaptive, creating its own workarounds to physical changes it encounters, both large and small.

There are many stories, for example, of people who lose an arm or a leg, but still feel pain in the missing limb. There are people who can access memories in their brains to the point that they can tell you exactly what happened on and what the weather was for every day going back twenty to thirty years.

In Danny's case, the damage was diffuse—spread throughout all areas of the brain. It was like a computer with an extremely nasty virus. And the effects began to show up very early in the developmental stages. His basic life functions are not affected, so his lungs, heart and glands function normally for the most part, except during seizures. His inability to lift himself to all fours, or crawl, or even walk, weren't because his muscles weren't developing. It was all about his balance and being able to make the millions of tiny snap decisions and choices that we normal humans take for granted just to function in our daily lives.

Through the program, we would train his body to respond appropriately to the external stimuli that his senses were constantly sending to his brain, which would give him the information he needed to exert control over his muscles to make intentional movements with his body.

We did things like strike his arms and legs repeatedly with a hard-bristled brush, softly at first but slowly increasing the force until he would flinch in pain. Once he flinched, we would praise him and move on to another activity.

We showed him hundreds of flash cards and spoke the name of the object on the card clearly and loudly in hopes that he would begin to make that connection. We especially did that with his food, hoping to use that basic need to build the first block toward receptive language.

Because the brain uses oxygen as food and requires it to grow physically, we would limit its most basic need by putting a specialized plastic mask over Danny's nose for a few seconds at a time, slowly increasing the length of the deprivation. The idea here was that the lungs would increase their size so they could store more oxygen for the brain to use during these disruptions.

This routine was repeated over and over and over again, all day and into the evening. Many times I found my wife and Danny asleep in our living room chair with various sensory stimuli scattered on the floor around them. They had both worked nonstop all day, only to collapse in exhaustion for a few hours rest before the next day began the process all over again.

Our team of rotating volunteers would take time out of their busy schedules to come to our home and help, mostly with the patterning, as that was the only part that required three people. The Institutes was adamant that this was the key to success for the entire program. Other parts of the routine could be skipped, but not patterning. They called it "external brain surgery."

The concept was that the brain develops a muscle memory for particular movements. That's why athletes shoot free throws, take endless batting practice or throw 500 footballs a day through a target. For the Institutes, developing these basic mental memories was the key to all brain development. They traced it back to the evolution of humans from crawling creatures (as babies) to stumbling toddlers to smooth walking and running adults.

All that began with the brain's development of a cross-pattern crawl (left hand and right knee forward, followed by right hand and left knee forward). So two adults would stand on either side of Danny as he lay on his back on a table and we would move his arms and feet in that manner, with another person turning his head from side to side in rhythm with the arm and leg movements, for five consecutive minutes (building eventually to fifteen-minute sessions). Danny didn't particularly enjoy having people forcing his arms and legs up and down, and he really hated having someone moving his head back and forth since he has an exaggerated sensitivity about anything touching his head. At times he would fight back, but at this point he was still too small to overcome three adults, although he did put up a pretty good fight late in the day when we were all exhausted.

It was boring, monotonous work, but at least it enabled us to spend hours in conversation with our team members (aka, very special friends). It made all the work bearable—at least for a while.

There were obvious improvements in Danny's abilities that excited and energized the whole team. When we began the program, Danny couldn't even get up on his hands and knees, much less crawl. We began his crawling program with a padded ramp that was set at such a steep angle that he barely had to move to slide down. With each trip to the bottom, we would reward him with a treat (a grape was the preferred trophy), record the amount of time it took him to make it down, lower the angle of the ramp a bit and start the process over.

In just a couple of weeks, the ramp was almost level, and Danny was using his arms and knees to propel himself from one end to the other.

The whole team rejoiced at that accomplished goal, and we redoubled our efforts, increasing the frequency and duration of the patterning and crawling activities, while letting some of the sensory issues fall by the wayside to make time in our overstuffed daily schedule.

The goal was to have Danny crawl a mile a day by the time we returned to Philadelphia for our follow-up visit in the summer. But we were progressing at breakneck speed. We would string grapes across the floor in our large home and he would hungrily crawl from treat to treat. We followed along with a rolling tape measure, recording each foot and resetting goals toward that 5,280-foot mark.

Someone bought Danny a remote-controlled car for Christmas, and we found it a great therapy tool, as he would follow the toy wherever we drove it, laughing maniacally all the way. The distances were growing by leaps and bounds every day.

It was an exciting time. We were surrounded by loving friends and family, and we were having great success at fixing our kid. There were occasional doubts and warnings offered by doctors and therapists that we should not get overly hopeful for the long-term prospects for Danny. They wanted us to be aware that Danny would probably never talk, or walk, or be anywhere near "normal," and to prepare ourselves to accept him as he was.

We chose to ignore them and just focus on the program. We were determined and we were seeing real fruit. God was obviously on our side, so no one was going to stop us. We even cut back on his weekly visits from the speech therapist and physical therapist because we couldn't spare the time from his program. This all seemed so logical. Danny didn't need to learn skills; he needed to develop his brain. Our program was obviously doing that, so the answer was simple. Do it with more frequency, intensity and duration.

This was the answer, and nothing—not friends, family, finances, exhaustion, our personal dreams and needs, not even the tedium of it all—was going to stop us now. We had found the way, and we were going to pursue it come hell, high water, death or Friday night football.

And winter turned into spring.

Chapter 3
A MAJOR LIFE CHANGE

"Many are the plans in a man's heart, but it is the Lord's purpose that prevails."

— Proverbs 19:21

*I*n the handicapped world, even the smallest advances are occasions for great celebration. With Danny making such amazing progress in his crawling, our families and friends began to catch the dream we had been casting ever since we had returned from Philadelphia. There *was* hope to fix Danny. He *would* walk someday. And even if he never talked, he *would* learn to communicate.

That was the mindset of everyone around us as we approached Danny's second birthday. The goal of crawling a mile a day had been met at a pace that stunned even his mother and me. We couldn't wait to return to the Institutes to get our next plan, to move on to the next stage. In fact, this thing was working so well, we decided to double down, to pull up stakes and move as close to Philadelphia as we could so that we could devote even more time and energy to this amazing program.

Our elated calls to the Institutes, though, were met with a disturbingly mild response and an admonition to not worry about the next step—just keep doing what you are doing. We couldn't put our fingers on it at the time, and we refused to focus too much on the negative vibes we sometimes got from the Institutes' staff, but something definitely didn't seem right. The other reality we didn't discuss, but couldn't miss, was the fatigue setting in with our team. They were still as sweet as ever about helping. They were faithful in showing up and fulfilling their duties. But you could see it in their faces. They had children and lives of their own, and they were spending a lot of time focused on our son instead. Of course, no one ever complained, but we were all looking for some relief.

And there was also the Chrissy issue that needed addressing. Our seven-month-old daughter spent most of her time in a playpen or in her car seat, parked next to the patterning table or in the adjoining room where she could receive attention during boring times of Danny's program. But she was becoming less patient with the leftover crumbs of time and energy we threw her way, and often demanded to be taken out of whatever device she was confined to and played with.

I think it was about that time that someone told us about the movie, *Lorenzo's Oil*. In the movie, Nick Nolte and Susan Sarandon portray a real-life couple whose son develops an extremely rare medical condition that threatens to take his life and doom him to incredible pain and misery in the process. The doctors offer little hope, so they decide to fight the battle on their own. The late Roger Ebert captured the movie, and the reality of many parents of handicapped children, in his glowing review posted on rogerebert.com:

"(Nolte and Sarandon) play a married couple sometimes too exhausted and obsessed to even be nice to one another. But they have a common goal. They want to save their son's life."

While Danny's condition wasn't life threatening, it was quality-of-life threatening—at least in our minds. We just knew there had to be an answer that would enable him to walk and talk and be just as normal as his little sister. It was our task to find that answer, and nothing was more important.

Even though we had concerns about the Institutes, it still offered the only hope we had found. In our enthusiasm and dedication, we determined that we would be the ones to take the Institutes' great work to the next level, to prove to the world that the program would work. And we would have a fixed Danny to show for it.

Thus began the quest to find the best place to raise our kids and pursue this worthy dream. It had to be someplace closer to Philadelphia than Texas, as we would need to be making trips to the Institutes at least twice a year. Plus, there were great research facilities on the East Coast, and the Angelman Foundation was based in Florida.

After looking at some opportunities in upstate New York and rural eastern Ohio, we decided that the best course would be in the mountains north of Atlanta where Danny's mom had relatives. It was only a twelve-hour drive from our family and friends in Texas; and it was about halfway to Philadelphia. By moving to a small town, we could find housing cheap enough to enable us to not worry so much about making a living and instead focus our energies on Danny.

Chrissy would benefit, too. At least that was what we assured ourselves and our doubtful life group members. It would be great for everyone. Being in a small town in the beautiful north Georgia mountains was a no-brainer. I think many of our group agreed that this was a no-brainer decision, but not in the way we imagined.

The move took up weeks of packing and driving and unpacking and more driving. During that time, we were unable to continue the program, which did not please the Institutes at all. They didn't care about our big dreams and our great plans. They were unimpressed that we were making these huge, long-term life decisions. Just do the program. And come see us in June.

Physically and financially, there was no way we could make that June appointment, so we rescheduled for later in the summer. We had purchased a large, old and pretty run-down home that needed lots of work just to make it suitable for living. The sale of our Texas home hit a snag, which left us in need of immediate income. That meant I had to find a job—any job—quickly. Our return trip to the Institutes had to be delayed indefinitely, until our finances recovered. Perhaps by spring things would be better, we told the frustrated scheduler in Philadelphia.

Within a few weeks, I had found a sales job at a furniture store, the beginning of an entirely new career path. We were still unpacking, trying to bring our monstrous old home with so many problems under control, and looking for local therapists and doctors for Danny.

Looking back on this tumultuous period with the advantage of twenty-five years of hindsight, it is amazing to see how foolish two intelligent adults can be, even with the best of intentions. But it is equally amazing to see how God can bless us during our follies. Even though we had relocated to a tiny, rural community, we had moved to one that already had two other Angelman Syndrome youths in the county. In fact, they were being treated by the pediatrician we found. The pediatrician was from India, where alternative medicine is accepted and promoted (which would make a huge impact on our lives, especially Danny's, in the years to come).

We found a wonderful, forward thinking, aggressive physical therapist who became a part of our family, teaching Danny how to walk (at least in the swimming pool), guiding my wife in her quest to find the best resources for Danny's ongoing development, and encouraging us to never give up or give in to the pessimism and easy answers we often got from other medical professionals.

In the midst of all the confusion, stress, financial worries, social adjustments and sheer exhaustion, we began to slowly take our eyes off the ball. We weren't doing the program anymore. We didn't have our support system anymore. We weren't seeing any great advances in Danny anymore. The hard reality was we didn't have a smooth, familiar routine around which we could fit family, friends and marriage anymore.

In many ways, the beginning of the end had come, but we were too busy to even notice. Prior to our move, we had a home-based marketing business, which meant I could be home every day to help with Danny's program and entertain Chrissy. More importantly, I could keep a close eye on my wife's struggles, encouraging her, relieving her when the program became too physically and emotionally exhausting, reminding her of the amazing good work she was doing when the results didn't come as quickly or as significantly as we had hoped.

Now I was gone for a huge part of every day, and I brought home a whole new set of worries and frustrations from my job. It stopped being about us. Now, little by little, day by day, my world became less about family and more about me.

In short, I traded my role as husband and father for one as breadwinner and weekend reliever. At the time, we both could and would give lots of reasons why this was a good trade. In fact, we could give you a few thousand reasons every month.

As summer turned to fall, I found myself in a job I truly hated, working on a house that had a never-ending list of things to fix, seeking that perfect balance that would enable us to get back to the plan we had perfected in Texas.

Our Texas house finally sold, and I was able to quit that hated job. But within a few months, we realized that the "new" old house would take any and all monies we were able to scrape together. Christmas that year was not a particularly happy one. We were still trying to do the program, but life kept getting in the way. Besides, Danny was still crawling, and he had found a great new activity swinging wildly in a small hammock on our side porch, getting lots of tactile stimulation and deep breathing exercises (from laughing maniacally as he twisted and turned in the swing for hours on end).

My wife began doing research into cell replacement therapy. She found a therapist in Atlanta who had a program that was very similar to the Institutes' program, only more family friendly. He was tied in with a doctor from England (at least he said he was a doctor) who had been having great success worldwide by injecting cells from sheep into humans. It was illegal to sell these sheep cells (say that five times fast) in the United States, but they could be purchased in Europe and shipped into the country. We met with the therapist and got a new program. We met with the English doctor and made plans to order some cells.

Our already suffering bank account took another blow. By January, we were desperately low on funds and there was a lot to be done on our house, especially with the cold winter upon us. I found a new job that was better than the previous one, but it required me to travel out of town for days on end every week. Still, I rationalized, this was good for my family. If I was able to make enough money, Danny and his sister would have their mom at home full time, and she really was the best one to manage his program and raise my daughter.

Another chink had been lodged in our family wall. Our goal was still the same—to fix Danny. The life we had found in Georgia wasn't all we had hoped it would be. In truth, it had been a pretty big disappointment for all of us and a step back for Danny's program. But we were determined. We would make this work, no matter what. We would adjust and be more diligent.

Adjusting is something parents of handicapped kids find themselves doing a lot. We find new doctors and new friends, as well as new ways of coping with our handicapped child, our normal child and our own brokenness. We become experts at making wrong decisions with the right intentions. We sacrifice our own sanity, finances and future in the hopes of meeting the special needs of our child. We learn to accept our child's disabilities, but deep down we still fight and pray that one day he will be different—that is, not so different from all the other kids.

We tell ourselves that God has chosen us to care for this special child, and that it is our Christian duty to do everything we can, to give everything we have, to make this right. We weep and call out to God for His strength and His guidance, but we lose sight of the bigger picture. Jesus' final commandment to his disciples was to love one another as He loved us—totally, without condemnation, without regard to our abilities or potential.

We were fighting the good fight, but we had lost sight of the battleground. It was all about fixing Danny. That was, we honestly believed, our God-ordained path. But in our obsession with helping Danny develop the skills that would help him live a quality life, we overlooked the most important responsibility and challenge for our whole family—to love him, and each other, unconditionally and intentionally.

Chapter 4
RIDING THE CRISIS COASTER

"Blessed are the poor in spirit, for theirs is the kingdom of God."
– Matthew 5:3

Like most personal crises and tragedies, discovering you have a handicapped child sends you through a series of stages: denial, discovery, despair, determination and, finally, acceptance. It all starts with denial. "Not my child" is the natural first reflex.

In many cases, the deformities are too obvious to ignore. More often, the issues are less clear and subject to debate by doctors, therapists, well-meaning family members and friends, your pastor, radio talk-show hosts, best-selling authors, and the lady behind you in the Express Lane at Walmart when you are just trying to get some diapers and get home at the end of a long, tiring day with an out-of-control kid.

Sometimes the evidence is there prenatally, leaving the parents with the horrible choice to abort the pregnancy or go forth with a painfully uncertain future.

When we first learned my wife was pregnant with Danny, we discussed several tests that the ob-gyn wanted to perform to determine the health of the baby. One of those was amniocentesis, a common but somewhat dangerous test used to detect potential genetic defects and other issues, which were of particular concern since my wife was beyond thirty-five years of age at the time.

"If you find something, would you be able to treat it?" I asked.

"No, but you could determine if you want to continue with the pregnancy or not," he calmly replied.

I remember being shocked and sickened at the thought of aborting this unborn human, my beloved child. I couldn't imagine making such a decision, but then, at that time I was totally ignorant of the severity of some types of handicaps. To be honest, I can't say what I would choose if I knew my unborn child would face a life of extreme physical hardships, operations, repeated long-term hospital stays, unquenchable pain or unseen and untreatable emotional demons.

I would like to say that as a devout Christian and believer in the sanctity of life I would always choose to honor God's gift. I can say that I have never, ever for a second regretted the decision to not even go down that road; that Danny's issues and challenges are nothing compared to the blessing he has been to me and to all who have encountered him.

But I would never presume to judge the choices others have made in the face of bringing a child into a lifetime of pain and perpetual treatment.

If I have learned anything about being a parent of a *special* child, it is that one of the greatest challenges is the reality of being "God" when it comes to your child's life. You make all the decisions, you call all the shots, you lose all the sleep worrying if you are doing it right. And there is no quick and easy reference to flip to for direction. You can Google a million ideas, resources, opinions, experiences—but at some point, the choice is yours and yours alone (emphasis on alone).

That really sucks sometimes. No, that really sucks most of the time.

One of the common complaints we heard a lot from parents (and experienced ourselves to a certain extent) is the plague known as "mother's intuitionitis." It goes this way. A new mother spends all her time and energy doting on and caring for her beautiful new baby. Naturally, she is hyper-aware of every minute change (or lack thereof), which she brings to the attention of her overworked and overbooked pediatrician at every appointment. "Oh, you are just being a new mother," is the often-condescending reply. "Your child is just a late bloomer. Every child develops at a different pace. Don't worry about it; your stress is more a threat to your child than any physical or mental issue at this young age."

And so it goes for the first two, three sometimes five or six critical years. Then, at some point, maybe even as the child struggles to keep up or adapt to preschool or kindergarten, more testing reveals that mom's intuition was right all along. There is something physically, mentally, emotionally or chemically wrong. Unfortunately, precious developmental time has passed, and the options are much more limited now than they would have been if the problem had been addressed during those critical first three years of a child's life.

Perhaps the cruelest words a mom can hear is "If we had only caught this earlier…"

With Danny, we experienced that with our first pediatrician, but dispensed with him quickly (after the six-month checkup). Our next pediatrician was a very sweet lady who had been a nurse when she gave birth to a physically handicapped child. Her frustration with finding a doctor who would take *her* child's issues seriously led her to go back to school and become a pediatrician.

This is one of those critical issues faced by parents of special children. Choosing a good doctor is vital to your sanity as you navigate these uncharted waters for your family. Surrounding yourself with a good support team of doctors, therapists, family and friends can make the difference in determining how productive and peaceful every other facet of your life is.

Because here is another reality that you need to accept—there WILL be times when you are going to screw this up. You are going to make bad decisions, you are going to choose selfishly, you are going to listen to the wrong advice, you are going to mail it in, you are going to miss the obvious.

If you have the right team around you, they will respect your decisions and support you no matter what. But they also are going to raise red flags, give you another point of view, ask the hard questions, remind you of the thing you have chosen to forget, encourage you to take a few deep breaths, sleep on it and not do anything rash.

That is the big mistake we made in choosing to leave our comfort zone in Texas and strike out on this new Fix Danny Adventure on our own. We made the choices we made with the best intentions, giving no quarter to the red flags and doubts raised by many of our closest friends and supporters. We went directly from denying that Danny had any serious long-term problems to denying that we couldn't fix it. We made our plan and married it for better or worse.

We took comfort in having made a decision, even if there might have been some lingering doubts. But here's the thing. That cycle of denial, discovery, despair, determination and acceptance isn't a one-time event. Just because you work through it and make peace with your new reality doesn't mean reality is satisfied to leave you alone. There are constantly new stresses, issues, challenges and disappointments that make you go back to square one and question everything. What did you miss? Was that decision the right one? What if you misheard God's answer to your prayers?

Add in a spouse who is going through this battle with you, and the chances for doubt and disagreement increase exponentially. Remember, you bring the knives of your own personality to this gun battle for your child's future. And your spouse brought his or hers. Some couples, the lucky and smart ones, use these cycles as opportunities to reevaluate their differences and strengthen their commonalities. They are honest enough about their own fears and inadequacies to allow their partners to stand in the gaps when they can't rely on their own intuitions and good intentions.

Like I said, those are the lucky and the smart ones. For the rest of us, these disruptions to our lives and our dreams often lead to resentment, discouragement, anger, distrust, self-pity and blaming. Our child's weaknesses and inabilities point out our own emotional infirmities. We can't blame the child for being the way he is, we don't want to blame God for making him that way, but we are hurt and angry and we just need to vent, either outwardly or inside our broken hearts and confused minds.

So we fight. And pout. And keep count of our spouse's faults and failures that keep popping up in every argument, discussion and decision. Eventually, we just go to our own corners and try to make the best of what we see is a very bad situation. In our case, since I was working and traveling, the decisions for Danny's day-to-day care fell to his mom. Besides, being the people pleaser and codependent personality that I am, it was easier to just accept the fact that she was right and I was wrong, and to just do what I could to support her and keep the peace.

We approached Danny's third birthday in a drafty 4,000-square-foot money pit, hundreds of miles between our support team back in Texas and our demanding new treatment partner in Philadelphia. I was on the road four or five days a week in my new sales management career, leaving my wife to oversee the work on our house, the ongoing therapy for Danny and the care of two-year-old Chrissy.

"This is just a temporary setback," we kept telling ourselves. "Once we get the downstairs renovated, and we catch up on some of these bills, we can focus more on Danny again. It's just a matter of time."

We were optimistic and excited about our new plan, even if the Institutes weren't at all happy about it. We weren't particularly happy with them, either, but believed that could be worked out once we got through this tough spot.

For Danny's part, he was just his usual good-natured, happy self. That's the thing about Angelman Syndrome. There are almost no physical issues, so there aren't a lot of medical crises or ongoing therapies required. There are no operations or long-term stays in the hospital. There are no feeding tubes or breathing treatments to deal with. At three, Danny wasn't really that far behind in his development, which was stuck at about eighteen months. We still had time, we figured. We just needed to get things a bit more organized and less hectic.

We weren't doing any of the program anymore, but he was getting physical therapy and he was highly stimulated in the swing on our side porch, and with all the freedom he found on our huge back deck and yard. He was very adept at crawling and fearless in his explorations. If he heard the neighbors across the street or the neighbor kids in the front yard or just a noisy bird in one of the giant oak trees that encircled our property, he would take off crawling as fast as he could go, right off the edge of the porch and into the flower bed two feet below.

The move may have left my wife and me struggling financially and doubting our decisions, and it may have caused our two-year-old daughter some anxiety as she had to adapt to a whole new environment and schedule, but Danny couldn't have been happier. He had lots of new places to roam, lots of new things to get into and a lot fewer demands put on him by adults who were always trying to put a mask over his mouth and nose, make him crawl when and where they wanted, or take control of his arms and legs as he lay helplessly on his back.

And home life wasn't totally bad. We did have a great old house with hardwood floors, high ceilings and amazing decks. Even though I was gone most of the week, the weekends were filled with raking leaves and playing in the piles or going to the beautiful state park and playing in the cold, clear creek or just cooking out with family. There may have been an ever-present undercurrent of worry and stress, but there was laughter and love.

We settled into the determination and acceptance phases of our journey with Danny. The past three years had tested our faith and our marriage mightily, but throughout it all we felt like we could always count on each other and on God. Admittedly, there were days when each of us had doubts and concerns about the other, but we had made it through a lot so far with no more damage than what we saw in other couples around us.

Besides, Danny and his sister were counting on us. This may not have been the life either one of us would have chosen, but it was the life we were given. For me, this was just a continuation of the life I had lived as a child on a farm with cows and crops that had to be cared for, regardless of how you were feeling that day. It is, as they say, what it is.

Or at least it was for a little while. And then it all took a new, and much scarier, turn for the worse.

Seizures.

Chapter 5
SEIZURES

Warning: The information presented in the next couple of chapters regarding seizures, including all comments regarding their diagnosis and treatment, should not be taken as medical advice. I am only recording my experiences of twenty-plus years ago. I am no doctor and every year brings new and better tools for dealing with seizures. If you suspect your child is suffering from seizures, contact your physician or the nearest emergency medical services immediately. While most seizures are not life-threatening, these are real medical events and real damage can occur if ignored.

"They dress the wound of my people as though it were not serious. 'Peace, peace,' they say, when there is no peace."
– Jeremiah 6:14

erriam-Webster offers this medical definition of seizures: 1: a sudden attack (as of disease); *especially*: the physical manifestations (as convulsions, sensory disturbances, or loss of consciousness) resulting from abnormal electrical discharges in the brain (as in epilepsy) 2: an abnormal electrical discharge in the brain.

"Sudden" and "attack" are definitely appropriate descriptions for seizures, not only for the person who is experiencing the seizure, but also for all those around him. We had been warned that one of the realities of Angelman Syndrome is that Danny would begin experiencing seizures around the age of three. We had done our research and thought we were prepared.

But nothing could have prepared us for the fear and sense of helplessness we felt as we watched our sweet boy writhe and shake and twitch uncontrollably. Nor did we expect the lack of clarity, advice or direction we received from our medical advisers. In fact, there seemed to be almost no agreement among them as to what constituted a seizure, how damaging it was and what the proper treatment should be.

On its website, The Epilepsy Foundation defines a seizure this way:

- The electrical activity is caused by complex chemical changes that occur in nerve cells.
- Brain cells either excite or inhibit (stop) other brain cells from sending messages. Usually there is a balance of cells that excite and those that can stop these messages. However, when a seizure occurs, there may be too much or too little activity, causing an imbalance between exciting and stopping activity. The chemical changes can lead to surges of electrical activity that cause seizures.

Even though seizures usually end on their own and cause minimal-to-no long-term damage, the Foundation warns that "people can injure themselves, develop other medical problems or life-threatening emergencies."

In short, seizures are not something to be ignored, especially when you see them for the first time. The good news is that with the internet, information about what you are really seeing in your child's behavior is only a click away. When we first started seeing them in the spring of 1995, the Internet was not nearly so developed or user friendly. And many of the symptoms of seizures were part of Danny's *normal* behavior. Things like lip-smacking or excessive drooling, poor balance, inattentiveness or lack of focus were things we saw in Danny every day.

Fortunately, we had been prepared for this, to a point, by his doctors and the information we had gotten from the Angelman Foundation. We were watching closely. And the behaviors that had become concerning to us took a giant leap in just a matter of weeks.

Which brings me to another one of those critical lessons we learned along the way: ***It is your kid, so trust your gut.*** I can't tell you how many times my wife and I had well-meaning, highly-trained professionals tell us that what we were seeing wasn't what we thought we were seeing, or that it wasn't important, or that there was nothing in the literature regarding this particular condition that would support our conclusion or concern.

Let me repeat this: ***It is your kid, so trust your gut.*** You are the expert on your child. You have been there and witnessed the nuances, the slight but important changes in his demeanor, the lifelessness in his eyes, the subtle twitch in the sides of his mouth. You know what is normal and what isn't for your child.

I'm not saying you should never listen to your doctor or be argumentative with him. In fact, I can attest to the ineffectiveness of arguing with medical professionals. They have their training and they cling to it. Sometimes they are exactly right. Be polite and respectful. But never stop watching your child. Never stop noting (and documenting) the things that concern you. Never stop researching and asking questions. And if the doctor refuses to answer your questions, find someone who will.

But I'm getting ahead of the story.

By Danny's third birthday, I had taken a sales job that required me to travel out of town from Sunday night until Friday afternoon, often several hundred miles from home. The seizures began during one of my first trips away.

There had been some questionable episodes in the weeks before, mostly drop seizures. Danny was crawling pretty well by this time, and he would be trucking right along when suddenly one of his arms would fling wildly straight out from his shoulder and he would take a nosedive into the hardwood floor. But these were isolated incidents, and Danny was still getting used to his new environment. He often would be crawling at breakneck speed across a slick floor, so maybe he had just slipped. Still, something didn't seem right.

By the time I left for my first sales assignment, my wife had documented a wide range of behaviors and incidents that looked like the whole spectrum of seizures: drop, myoclonic, tonic-clonic, petit mal. At first, they seemed to hit without warning, but then we noticed that Danny would stop whatever he was doing and lay down on his side before they hit. We determined that he could feel them coming on and didn't want to repeat the face planting experience. Sometimes after the seizures, he would cry (which was odd for Danny) and he would be warm to touch.

His mom began documenting the type, frequency and duration of these episodes, along with the warning signs and after-effects. She shared those with his pediatrician, therapists and the Institutes. Their responses were interesting and highly instructive into how the medical world often works.

The pediatrician's response was that seizures can be a serious medical emergency and must be treated aggressively with drugs, although the fact that the patient was a three-year-old nonverbal child with a rare genetic disorder posed some definite challenges when it came to determining the right drug and the right dosage. We would have to pick one, start with a relatively low dosage, and keep increasing it until the problem was under control.

Just as there is a wide spectrum of seizure types and effects, there is an equally wide range of seizure medications with all sorts of effectiveness (many are good as stopping them immediately, but the body adapts to them in a matter of weeks, meaning that dosages must be constantly adjusted) and side effects. Common side effects are drowsiness, loss of attention, irritability, drooling, nausea, even liver and bone damage.

The Institutes didn't believe in seizures. Yawns are seizures, they told us. Even the Epilepsy Foundation said that most seizures are not harmful. Introducing drug therapy for seizures would conflict with the program they had prescribed, the Institutes' argued, and that was unacceptable. Putting Danny on any kind of drugs would seriously impact his treatment and violate the agreement we had made with them. Just keep doing the program and let the seizures run their natural course.

As much as we hated the thought of putting Danny on a drug therapy regimen (something we had seen other parents of handicapped kids do and had sworn we would never allow), we couldn't escape the reality of Danny laying lifeless in our arms, his hands and mouth twitching uncontrollably, unresponsive to our pleadings to come back to us, eyes darting wildly from side to side, body almost too hot to touch.

And so comes another opportunity in the journey of raising a handicapped child where you get to play God. It is a lonely and despairing place to be. Your doctors and other health advisers are passionate in their beliefs and have plenty of facts and experiences to back up their position.

But you are the one holding your sweet child. I don't believe a person can look more helpless and dependent than when they are in the middle of or just coming out of a seizure. It isn't something I can adequately describe. And when that person is a three-year-old child, in fact, *your* three-year-old child, well…

The doctor had warned that failure to control seizures could result in additional damage to his brain or even to his body (since the brain controls all the other body functions). They could even cause death.

We had picked up our lives, moved 800 miles, bought a large fixer-upper home, left behind dear friends and family, spent almost all the money we had accumulated—all to pursue a dream of working with a program that held the only promise we had for "fixing" our son. And now, we were on the verge of cutting all ties with them and starting all over—again—with no Plan B waiting in the wings.

Despite this crisis, life marched on. I had a job and we desperately needed the money that job provided. As a couple, we were severely limited in the amount of time and energy we could spend together working on this soul-challenging decision. We debated the matter endlessly on the phone, as I sat each evening in a hotel room on the Atlantic Coast eight hours away. My wife stayed on the front lines of that battlefront while I took a rear position. Neither of us was happy about that, but just like on the dairy farm of my youth, life in the real world goes on regardless of the crisis of the day.

We cried. We fought. We comforted and assured one another. But we didn't reach a conclusion.

Danny did that for us. His seizures finally reached a point where he required immediate medical attention, so his mom took him to the local hospital, and he was admitted. In most emergency rooms, the drug of choice for controlling seizures is some sort of tranquilizer, like Ativan or Clonazepam. It seems that if the seizure event can be stopped, the brain has a chance to reset, the chemical imbalances correct themselves, at least temporarily, and everything goes back to "normal" until the next event.

The medication did the trick, although the side effects were pretty severe. He slept a lot and was listless when he was awake, but at least the seizures were under control. I came home early from that week's assignment and we spent time encouraging one another and trying to prepare ourselves for the next step. Once again, we had made it through another major crisis, clinging to one another and to God. We had taken another ride on the emotional roller coaster through the dips of despair and doubt, and the high arcs of hope and discovery. We had returned with more determination and acceptance for this new chapter in our crazy lives.

With the seizures temporarily under control, all we had to do was get the correct long-term drug identified and the dosage adjusted. Then we could move forward. But first, we had to notify the Institutes of our new plans. They were adamant that he shouldn't be on seizure medication, and we were equally adamant that they could go straight to –well, let's just say we parted ways with the Institutes.

We had thrown in with the doctors, but not completely. We still weren't thrilled with the idea of Danny being on a drug regimen, and we were determined to keep looking for alternatives. But where?

Chapter 6
A BRUSH WITH DEATH

"My God, my God, why have you forsaken me? Why are you so far from saving me, so far from my cries of anguish? My God, I cry out to you by day, but you do not answer. By night, but I find no rest."
– Psalm 22:1-2

O ne of the challenges of dealing with a child's disability is the temptation of the easy answer and half solution. There are so many issues to deal with and so many choices to make (with few clear cut options and lots of gray area for second-guessing and doubt), once a path is chosen, it is hard not to just go with the flow and let someone else take the helm for a while.

Even though the seizure issue had pushed us to the Point of No Return with the Institutes, there were ideas they had planted in our lives that had taken deep root and would continue to influence our decisions. We may have disagreed on the need for medication to control the seizures, but we weren't ready to simply accept whatever choices the doctor made.

For the first few months following Danny's third birthday, his mom and the doctor researched, discussed, argued about and endlessly sought the right drug and the right dosage for Danny. For his part, Danny rode the medication roller coaster, going from pretty good seizure control to days and nights of endless episodes, all dutifully recorded and timed by his mom.

It was a tense time for the entire family, but life goes on, even during times of trouble and fear, so I headed back out on the road to try to keep the family financially afloat, and the work continued on the house. In a matter of weeks, I was promoted to Regional Vice President of Sales in my company, which meant a significant pay increase, but also a summer-long stint back in Texas getting training of my own, then training others all over the state.

The company flew me home every other weekend, but 800 miles away from your family is a great distance, even in the best of circumstances. Our circumstances were far from best, and about to take a serious turn for the worse.

When I checked into the Holiday Inn in Tyler for my latest assignment, a message was waiting for me, along with the salesman I was supposed to spend the next three days training. The message was brief and horrifying: Call home immediately.

My wife informed me that Danny had been in the hospital since late the night before, and they were unable to break his very high temperature. In fact, it was reaching life threatening proportions. They had tried everything, all to no avail. Each passing hour dramatically increased the possibility of physical and mental damage, and if they couldn't break the fever—well, it didn't look good.

Part of the problem parents of handicapped kids face in these times of medical crisis is the necessity to constantly educate and direct every nurse, therapist and physician your child encounters about the idiosyncrasies of the particular illness, disability or defect that defines your child medically. Angelman Syndrome is still pretty rare, although more cases are identified every year.

Before the genetic testing gave Danny's reality a name, the doctors were about to hang the diagnosis Cerebral Palsy on him. That is the generic, umbrella term preferred when there is no other definitive syndrome identified, and it makes sense. Cerebral means brain related, and palsy means paralysis accompanied by involuntary tremors.

Every time there was a shift change at the hospital and a new nurse or resident came in to check Danny's chart and take over his care, his mom would have to go through her two-minute primer on what Angelman Syndrome is, how it affects the body, what needs to be watched for and what treatments are usually a waste of time, energy and Medicaid money.

The doctors had just tried something else when I called to check on him; I have no idea what it was. All I knew was my son's life was literally hanging by a thread and I was stuck in a hotel 800 miles away from home, and 100 miles from the airport. I called my boss and told him that I was expecting a phone call in about an hour, and if the news wasn't good, I would be headed back to Dallas to catch the first flight to Atlanta. I gave my trainee some material to study for the afternoon, and I went to my room, where I sat in the dark, weeping and praying.

Finally the call came and the news was good: the fever had broken. There was no way of knowing if any damage had been done to Danny's three-year-old body or brain, but at least he was out of danger—for now.

I made arrangements to fly home the next day and crammed two days of training into one afternoon and evening session.

One of the things that had been drilled into us at the Institutes was that the brain—even an undeveloped one like Danny's—does most of its growing in the first five years of life. After age five, growth can still occur, but at a much, much slower rate. When you have a kid whose brain is lagging, time is of the essence.

What I found when I arrived home was more troubling than anything I had imagined, short of death. Danny was home from the hospital and was laying on his bed. And that is all he was doing. Laying there. No eye movement, no recognition of me or anyone else, no whining or fussing, no laughter. He was just a lifeless lump.

The doctors had found the fix for the immediate problem, and the seizures and the high temperatures had broken. But the drugs used to achieve that life-saving result had left us with a sad shell of our son. There were obviously adjustments to be made to find the right dosage, but we had already been warned that this drug wouldn't be the long-term answer because its effectiveness would wear off within a few weeks. The search would continue to find what, if anything, would give us back our son, handicapped but full of life.

And at that moment, I experienced that horrible question that I suspect many parents of special needs kids face at some point—Does this person have any quality of life? I write this nearly twenty-five years after the experience, and I can still remember that bitter coldness that swept over me. Were we fighting a losing battle, and were we doing Danny any favors by fighting so hard?

I remember bits and pieces of the discussion I had with my wife that night, much of it in tears and pitched voices, about what had been going on and what the right thing to do would be. I can be a fairly negative person at times, and this was one of those times when I immediately began voicing my worst doubts and fears.

Fortunately for all of us, his mom had done enough research to know this didn't have to be the end. In fact, her personality led her to double down during times of great stress, to look harder and ask more questions and dig her heels in no matter what the "experts" told her.

Here is another of those hard truths about the special needs world: most of the doctors and medical professionals you encounter don't have the experience or training to truly understand your child's need. Remember, your child is not the norm, and is quite possibly the first patient with this disability that your doctor has ever seen. It seems that American doctors, especially those with M.D.s, have a background that is strongly based in drugs and procedures aimed at treating specific symptoms.

Most of the medical professionals you will meet will be polite and accommodating. A few will be very interested and thankful for the information. Some will resent the input from a nonprofessional, over-zealous parent trying to play doctor. Fortunately, those are few and far between, but they are there, like our original pediatrician and one of the doctors Danny's mom encountered during this crisis.

Danny had been in a state of nonstop seizures for several hours and nothing that the doctors at our rural hospital tried could stop them or bring his fever down. During the night, one particularly obstinate doctor "knew" exactly what the problem was and how to treat it.

"Well it's pretty obvious what is going on here," he had proclaimed within a minute of reviewing Danny's chart, and began making suggestions to the nurse on what drugs needed to be administered at once. Danny's mom stepped in and explained that course of action had been tried before in a previous trip to the hospital, and gave reasons why it didn't work.

The doctor scowled, didn't respond directly to her input at all, but immediately suggested another route that would surely work. "No,"

Danny's mom responded. "That won't work either. We've tried that before too."

"Well," he huffed, "I guess you're beat before you even get started. If those won't work, nothing will." He handed the chart to the nurse, wheeled around and sauntered out the door and onto the next patient's room, leaving behind a three-year-old child fighting for his life and a middle-aged mom fighting for her hope and her sanity.

Doctors and nurses have their training and they cling to it. And let's face it—our kids are *different*. The reality of modern medical care is that it is driven by the need to see as many patients as possible in order to cover the ever-burgeoning costs of equipment, offices, trained staff and malpractice insurance. Our kids often require a larger than normal amount of personalized care and in-depth research. Unfortunately, most of them are covered by Medicaid, which limits severely the rate of pay physicians can expect for that care.

So they fall back on their basic training, which for most M.D.s means prescribing and managing drug therapy. They just don't have the time or resources to do anything else.

This seems to be less true of D.O.s (osteopathic doctors), who are trained to take a more holistic approach to treatment plans. That would include various physical and occupational therapies, nutrition and alternative medicines. By nature, this type of treatment requires the doctor to work as a team member with the parent and various therapists. That fact alone can result in a significant change in your outlook on the battles you inevitably face as the parent of a special needs child.

Don't misunderstand—I have known bad D.O.s and great M.D.s. I'm just pointing out that this most critical member of your care team should be chosen carefully—which usually isn't an option when you are dealing with doctors on call and on staff in emergency rooms.

But as we found throughout our fix-Danny quest, God always provided the right answer and the right people to help us to the next step if we were diligent enough in our research and prayers, and if we were patient. In the small north Georgia community where we had settled, we found a pediatrician who had been trained in India, where holistic medicine and alternative treatment methods were widely accepted and encouraged.

Even in this remote, rural section of Georgia, there were at least two other Angelman Syndrome children, so the doctor was familiar with our challenge. And he was highly encouraging for my research-obsessed wife, who would spend hours poring through any and all medical information she could locate on the Internet or in books she acquired through friends and therapists.

If there was an alternative to drug therapy for seizure disorder, she was determined to find it. And she had the right team surrounding her to make it happen.

As it turned out, we found the answer to Danny's seizures not in drugs, but in butter, mayonnaise, high fat hot dogs and macadamia nuts. We had already experienced one miracle in Danny's increased mobility through the Institutes' program. We were about to witness yet another one in the Ketogenic Diet.

Chapter 7
A DIFFERENT PATH TO HEALTH

"You will know the truth. And the truth will set you free."
– John 8:32

Before we get into the details of our experience with the Ketogenic Diet, perhaps this would be a good time to discuss the whole wide (and wild) world of Alternative Medicine. As already noted, your run-of-the-mill pediatrician gets very little training or experience in dealing with special needs children. Their focus is on treating the many normal illnesses most children confront and, as with most other specialists, the more patients they can see in a day, the better their bottom line.

Over time, many parents get tired of getting unsatisfactory answers to their many questions in the care of their handicapped children, so they begin to look elsewhere. They look hard at nutrition. And physical therapy. And kinesiology. And homeopathy. And cell therapy.

When we began our quest for the right fix for Danny, we were seeking whatever pill or treatment or procedure we could find that would jump-start his brain and allow him to catch up with the rest of the world. Doctors had offered little hope beyond just treating health issues as they arose, and when one did come up (seizures), their answer left us with a terribly lethargic and almost lifeless child.

The Institutes for the Achievement of Human Potential, a poster child for the promise of alternative medicine, had given us amazing results and hope—up to a point. But they were so unbending in their approach to serious seizure issues and their program was so demanding and time consuming, we finally felt the returns had diminished to a point where continuing with them would be detrimental not only to Danny's health, but to our family's overall well-being.

But that experience had convinced us of the value of non-traditional treatment programs. Through a series of contacts, we located a therapist formerly associated with the Institutes who had started his own consulting business working with families in exactly our predicament. His program was designed to mesh with our existing family reality, and it allowed room for inclusion of drug therapy for the seizures.

He also introduced us to a doctor from England, who traveled the world promoting the use of cell injections to help the brain regenerate itself and complete those missing connections that were at the root of Danny's developmental issues. The cells came from sheep, and since they were not approved by the FDA to be produced or sold in the United States, we had to have them shipped in from Germany or Mexico.

I remember they were expensive and came in a plain brown box. Once we received them, we then had to find someone who would inject these illegal and basically unknown substances into our three-year-old child. A nurse friend said yes, then backed out when she learned that she could lose her license if the authorities ever found out.

We thought we could do it and practiced giving injections to oranges. But sticking a needle in a piece of fruit doesn't compare to doing so to a squirmy three-year-old, and neither his mom nor I were up to the task. If it had been a life-or-death situation, then I have no doubt we could have overcome our discomfort. But to be honest, I wasn't at all sure this was a good idea.

You get that feeling a lot when you are making these kinds of gray decisions for your handicapped child.

Eventually, we found an alternative medical professional who agreed to do the deed. It was actually very anticlimactic (Danny tended to laugh when stuck with needles; inappropriate pain response is part of the Angelman Syndrome symptomatology). We watched Danny closely over the next few weeks, waiting for some amazing change. At first, it seemed as if this crazy idea might just work. The seizures and tremors stopped completely for the next few weeks but returned with a vengeance before the next round of injections. In fact, they seemed to be getting progressively worse. This experimental treatment had to be shelved while the focus turned back to finding the right medication to control the seizures without destroying Danny's quality of life.

I include this story to show the extremes to which you will be tempted to go to help your child. You will spend money you don't have, trust people you don't know, try things that sound absolutely crazy (and come with dire warnings from medical professionals and concerned family and friends). In short, you will be tempted to throw experience, intelligence and reason to the wind—anything to help your child.

Unfortunately, there are a lot of people out there who have no qualms in preying on your desperation to peddle their *miracle cure*. There are natural herbal remedies, essential oils, newly found chemical combinations, long-ignored treatments that were used "thousands of years ago by Native Americans"—you name it, someone has a website offering it at an "amazing low price."

As I was writing this more than twenty years after the fact, I was shocked to learn just how out there this treatment was. I had been thinking this was stem cell therapy, which has been controversial mostly for its use of live stem cells taken from aborted fetuses. But this was not that at all. It was cell therapy, a practice developed in the nineteenth century which showed little effectiveness in itself, but did result in the development of bone marrow transplant therapy.

Wikipedia was not available at the time we wandered into this little-known area of alternative medicine, but I will share with you what it says now about cell therapy. "This practice, according to the American Cancer Society, is not backed by any medical evidence of effectiveness, and can have deadly consequences."

As one who had spent way too much time and money chasing far too many quick fixes, let me offer this advice: ***Don't be afraid to try anything, but protect yourself. Protect your child's health***—which means do your research and use your common sense. With the all-inclusive reach of the modern Internet, answers can be no more than a few hundred mouse clicks away.

Remember: The more unbelievable a treatment's results sound, chances are the less likely you will enjoy any success. But it doesn't hurt to try (or it shouldn't). Just be very careful to know the possible side effects.

Protect your finances. As I will address later in this book, your finances can be a much bigger threat to your family and to you as a parent than any problems your child's disability can produce. You are a family with a handicapped child; don't become a handicapped family by letting your child's issues consume all your resources.

Finally, protect your heart. This is a marathon, not a sprint. The reality is that this disability is probably something you and your child will be dealing with until the end of both of your lives. There will be hard times ahead. (By the way, this is exactly the same reality faced by families with so-called "normal" kids. They may not have to deal with seizures or mental delay, but they have a never-ending struggle with bullying, low self-esteem, poor decision-making and broken hearts.)

This is not to condemn all forms of cutting-edge medical procedures and treatments. Quite the contrary. You should always have an open mind and an inquisitive spirit. Technology, especially when it comes to gene therapy—introducing DNA into cells to treat or prevent certain diseases and disorders—has advanced tremendously in the past twenty-five years. Already it is being studied at hospitals around the world and there are large corporations pouring millions of dollars into this research.

If a disease or a disability can be traced to its genetic origins, the DNA could theoretically be corrected prior to birth to prevent the problem before the baby is born, thus preventing future parents from making hard and costly decisions about their child's long-term care.

But what about fixing someone like Danny by altering his DNA now? I don't know, but I am not depending on it or placing any hopes on that at all. Medical research is about money and return on investment. Trials are incredibly expensive and take years to complete. The demand for genetic therapy will be in those health areas that affect the most people—things like cancer and metabolic diseases. More demand translates into more potential sales and greater return on investment.

Angelman's, like most other syndromes, affects a miniscule number of individuals worldwide, so the demand is small. Plus, the future of gene therapy bears the additional burden of overcoming political and ethical challenges. Perhaps someday there will be a treatment that will make my son "normal," but probably not in my time here. Or Danny's.

You can be frustrated and depressed and indignant about all this, or you can make the best of it. That doesn't mean just throwing up your hands and not trying to better your child's life. One thing we learn early on when caring for a disabled child is to cherish and celebrate the small steps, the miniscule changes. My son likely will never be able to go for a walk around the block or have a conversation with a close friend, but he loves to be outside enjoying nature and he loves to be around people, especially children.

His favorite time of the week is Sunday morning, sitting in the giant lobby of our church, watching the people stream in. Many make a point to come by to say hi or give him a quick pat on the back (don't linger too long or he will grab a fistful of shirt, hair or something embarrassing). The children come over to him, giving him wide berth but studying him ever so closely, trying to figure out what is up with this person who is as large as their parents, but is acting with a freedom that they understand and envy. Amazingly, while Danny can be rough and inappropriate with adults, he is always very tender, almost coy, with children.

The point is that there is more to your child than his or her disabilities. Yes, you never give up seeking out any treatments that might make life better or easier for him. You build a team of doctors, teachers and therapists who are supportive and open-minded about helping you achieve that goal. Don't believe everything you hear or read, but don't discount it without doing due diligence and knowing the truth for yourself.

The best thing you can do for your special needs child (and all your other children) is to never lose hope or sense of the big picture. And a critical part of that picture is ALL the people in it. That includes your handicapped child (both as he is and how he probably will be ten years from now), your spouse, your other children, close relatives and friends, medical professionals, teachers, therapists, insurance case managers, and representatives from the state agencies that help direct and fund your child's care.

I repeat—one of the biggest problems faced by parents of handicapped children is the sense of loneliness, especially if you are a single parent. It is easy to feel overwhelmed and totally beat down by just the routines of daily life, which are so much harder when you are having to bathe, diaper, feed, dress and provide twenty-four-hour care for another person.

But you are not alone. Step back and look at all the help you have around you (even though they aren't with you for those 2:00 a.m. diaper changes). Now take another step back and see that there is a plan in place for your life—that there is a Creator who made both you and this imperfect child and loves you both immeasurably. Take one more step back and look behind you to where you were when this all began, what you have come through since then, all the miracles and blessings that have fallen your way along with the struggles. It is easy to get so caught up in the routine and monotony of the daily battles that we miss the real beauty and joy of this special life to which you have been called.

All of our children—all of them, handicapped or not—are gifts from God. They are to be encouraged, celebrated and loved unconditionally. Yes, you have some special issues to confront, but you do that best when you are strong, resilient and optimistic.

Now, about that Ketogenic diet.

Chapter 8
THE KETOGENIC DIET

"He poured his grace on us. By giving us great wisdom and understanding, he showed us the mystery of his plan."
– Ephesians 1:8-9

Why? That's a common question for parents of special needs kids—as well as parents of "normal" kids. We all want to know the reasons behind our children's behavior or defining traits. Because knowledge brings some level of power and control over future development, or at least needed adaptation and acceptance.

Why is my kid not crawling? Why does he have seizures? Why can't he talk? Why can't we find the right treatment for this particular issue? Why isn't this drug working?

We try not to ask (at least out loud) those big, heavy "why" questions. Like, "why did this happen to me and my kid?" Or even "why did God do this?"

When Danny began having seizures shortly before his third birthday, our question really wasn't why. We knew the reason—one of the common manifestations of Angelman Syndrome is seizure disorder. It made perfect sense. Angelman's is a genetic defect which results in poor development of the brain's wiring, and since the brain controls everything in the body, misfiring axons and neurons would ultimately affect the proper functioning of nerves, organs, glands, circulatory and respiratory systems, and muscles.

In the space of a few months, Danny exhibited every possible type of seizure, including drop seizures, tonic, clonic, tonic-clonic, petit mal and, the baddest of them all, grand mal. He would be crawling across the floor and suddenly one of his arms would fling wildly to his side and he would face plant the floor. He would twitch and shake. His eyes would go dead—or dart wildly in all directions. His face would contort. He would gag. His body would be almost too hot to touch.

The medicines they gave him to control the seizures would result in behavior as difficult to witness as the seizures—sometimes more so. Phenobarbital was the original drug of choice, and it definitely succeeded in stopping the tremors. It also left him with almost no visible signs of life except for the nearly imperceptible rising and falling of his chest from his shallow breathing.

His eyes were dead, and he was totally unresponsive to anything, from our pleading voices to hand claps next to his ears to loud bangs. Our tears fell on a mere shell of the always laughing and active little boy we loved so much.

Our original quest to fix Danny took a new, more focused turn. We were determined to find the right dosage of the right medication to bring our son back to a real, quality life. Because even with all his developmental delays, he *did* have a life. He was happy and energetic and could be a real challenge to keep up with at times. He couldn't walk, although he was certainly making great progress in reaching that goal before the seizures began. He could crawl faster than some people could walk—so fast, in fact, that he often was off the front porch, across the street and into our neighbor's yard before we noticed (much to our horror and guilt).

Fortunately, we had found an important ally in our battle against the seizures. Even though we had moved to a tiny rural community in far north Georgia, we had been blessed with a wonderful, caring pediatrician who had received his medical training in India. That background had exposed him to many different approaches to care beyond standard drug therapy. He had no problem with our exploration of alternative medical treatments, and he wasn't so arrogant as to believe only he had the answers to our unique problems.

Along that line, he made a life-changing referral for Danny and our family as a whole. He put us in contact with the neurology department at Children's Medical Center in Atlanta. As critical as I often am of the medical profession when it comes to dealing with special needs, I must say that the experiences we had with the neurologists at children's hospitals in Atlanta and in Fort Worth, Texas, were nothing short of amazing.

At Children's in Atlanta, we went through yet another round of diagnostic tests, completed dozens of medical forms and answered hundreds of questions about every aspect of Danny's life from the time he was conceived. I must confess here that I am using the royal "we." I was on the road constantly with my job, so this tedious task fell to

Danny's mom, who also had a two-year-old daughter to care for at each step along the way.

This is important for parents of special needs kids to remember. There may be nothing more important than making sure that your special child receives the proper diagnoses and treatment plans. But that in no way diminishes the need to make sure each parent is being cared for and supported. That applies to the parent (usually the mom) who is on the front line and to the parent who has to go out and do battle with the world each day, leaving his beloved family behind to earn the money to keep them afloat. Nor does it decrease one bit the amount of love and attention your other children need.

Luckily (assuming you believe in luck, although I lean more toward God's divine hand at work), one of the neurologists at Children's had some recent experience with a new treatment for seizures. It was not based on any of the many drugs that were available (most of which we had already tried). Instead, it was based on a radical diet plan—the Ketogenic Diet.

During the writing of this book, I learned the truth of just how "lucky" (or blessed by a loving and gracious God) we really were. This diet had originally been developed in the 1920s as a treatment for pediatric epilepsy and had been used for the decade to follow. But the development of anticonvulsant drugs (like phenobarbital) had lessened its usage. In the mid-1990s (precisely the time when Danny turned three and began experiencing seizures), Jim Abrahams, a Hollywood film writer, director and producer best known for the *Airplane* movies, had a son named Charlie whose seizures were controlled by the diet.

Abrahams was so pleased with the success of this treatment he created the Charlie Foundation to promote research and public education about the diet. Our son was in the right hospital at the right time with the right doctor who gave us the information to pursue, finally, the right plan of attack against the seizures that were stealing his life.

If you are familiar with the Atkins Diet, or any high-fat, low-carb diet, you know the Ketogenic diet well. Carbs such as bread, starchy fruits and vegetables, sugar and grains are extremely limited or eliminated completely. Instead, the person is given a steady diet of high-fat foods, including butter, mayonnaise, hot dogs and nuts (macadamia nuts in particular).

Ordinarily, the body gets the energy it needs by turning carbohydrates from our diet into glucose and burning that. When there aren't enough carbs in the diet to provide sufficient supplies of glucose, the body makes chemicals called "ketones" from stored fat and burns those ketones for energy. There doesn't seem to be a clear answer on how this affects seizures, but it may be related to the production of a fatty acid, decanoic acid, during this process.

Whatever the reason, when the body is running off your stored fat, you lose weight rapidly and seizure activity drops precipitously.

We were told that if Danny could tolerate this diet for twenty-four months, not only would his seizure activity decrease significantly during that period, but the seizures would never return at the level previously experienced. He would still need anticonvulsant drugs, but in much smaller dosages with fewer, less drastic side effects.

We gathered all the material we could find on the right foods and the right portions. We stocked our fridge and our cupboard with lots of unhealthy, high-fat foods. We braced ourselves for battling Danny to get him to eat this type of diet (although that didn't come for a few months because this was something new, tasty and different from what he had been eating).

And, just as we had found in the early days of our Institutes treatment plan, the alternative medicine approach worked miracles. Danny's seizures declined drastically and immediately—in frequency, severity and duration. In short order, we reduced his medication. Still no serious seizure breakthroughs.

Best of all, the old Danny came back to us. He laughed. He crawled at breakneck speed. He pulled himself up on the sofa. He waved his arms when excited and played for hours on the porch swing.

For the next twenty-three months, the Ketogenic Diet ruled at our house. Danny eventually got tired of the same old, high-fat hot dogs smeared in mayonnaise and the spoonsful of real butter we forced on him every day, but we made it. Finally, one month before the two-year plan was up, Danny threw up his hands and absolutely refused to eat another bite of this miracle diet.

The results were exactly as promised. There have been almost annual breakthrough episodes, usually occurring when he is suffering some other illness, such as strep throat, swine flu or severe sinusitis. Some of these outbreaks have been severe and have resulted in short term hospitalization. But seizures became temporary issues, not ongoing struggles.

Don't just take my word for it. According to the Epilepsy Society's website, "a clinical trial at Great Ormond Street Hospital in 2008, and other studies since then, showed that the diet significantly reduced the number of seizures in a proportion of children whose seizures did not respond to AEDs. After three months, around 4 in 10 children who started the diet had the number of their seizures reduced by over half and were able to reduce their medication."

For us, this was huge. Not only were we able to get a true life-threatening risk removed from Danny's long list of challenges, with the seizures behind us we were able to turn our attentions back to doing those things that were making a difference in his development, like his weekly sessions with the physical therapist.

As I write this, Danny just turned twenty-seven, and he is on a minimal dosage of seizure medication, given only as needed when his seizure threshold drops due to other health issues. He has breakthrough seizures a couple of times each year, but they are mild and easily resolved.

The only long-term negative effect I have seen from the Ketogenic Diet was his distaste for high-fat foods (like butter and mayonnaise), and it has only been within the last couple of years that he quit turning up his nose at and refusing to take even one bite of a hot dog.

The seizure era was finally over for Danny and our family. It was the only serious health threat we ever had to face, and it gave me a great appreciation and empathy for those sad parents who I saw wandering the halls at the children's hospitals, putting up a brave face for their sick child and collapsing into a loved one's arms when the child was wheeled away for yet another treatment or procedure.

Danny had survived the worst part of the journey. And so had we—at least for a while.

*Danny and Chrissy found a temporary "new normal" when
Danny entered the school system in Georgia and Chrissy
was enrolled in a daycare academy where she could interact
with children her age and appropriate development.*

Chapter 9
SCHOOL

"Let wise people listen and add to what they have learned. Let those who understand what is right get guidance."
— Proverbs 1:5

The school hallways were wide, and every sound echoed off the tile floors and the painted cinder block walls. On each side stood a line of short humans, squirming and shuffling back and forth in small circles as they did their best to stand still and quiet.

These were the bus kids going through their afternoon routine of waiting as the teachers prepared themselves for the ten minutes of chaos that were about to ensue as the kids were herded by class out to the line of yellow buses. The non-bus riding kids were still in the classrooms, so these kids were under strict orders to wait in silent calm for about three more minutes.

When I walked in I half expected there to be a stir because kids in line are always looking for any excuse to break arbitrary rules and constraints. But they were too engrossed in their whispering, poking and giggling to notice a stranger in their midst.

I was there to pick up Danny for an early therapy appointment and as soon as I walked into the gathering storm of children, I saw him. Fortunately, he didn't see me, which would have brought out a loud laugh or squeal of excitement. That was one thing we knew about Danny—two things, actually. We knew that his vision was strong, and that he recognized and responded to familiar faces.

As part of the endless testing we had done early in this quest to determine what skills Danny might possess, we had taken him to an optometrist. The results were ridiculously inconclusive because the expectations were ridiculous.

After all, how was he to respond to questions about what he could or could not see on a screen when he was nonverbal? And there was no way the doctor was going to get him to look through that expensive Viewmaster-like tool he used on everyone else. We wrestled him down to let the doctor look deep into his eyes, but the bright light just drove him to shake his head violently back and forth and shut his eyes as tightly as possible.

A couple of days later, during one of the crawling sessions at home, we got the answer. To entice Danny to add distance to his crawling each day and eventually reach that one-mile mark, we would leave grapes on the floor and he would frantically crawl from grape to grape. Only one got overlooked. We were sitting in the den and Danny immediately turned from the path we were trying to get him to follow and headed straight for the front door. By the time I got up off the floor where I was sitting to steer his remote-control car that would lead him on the morning's journey, Danny had already moved off the carpeted area and onto the tile entryway. He reached the grape just before I got there—evidently it had been accidently kicked into a corner, and he had seen it out of the corner of his eye as he was heading through the living room toward his bedroom down the hall. Obviously, his vision worked just fine, even peripherally.

Danny not noticing me when I entered the school building turned out to be a wonderful gift of a memory and a quick insight in the value of school for him and his fellow students. Danny's group was near the front of the line of kids on the right side of the hall. He didn't see me because a group of teachers stood at the door in front watching the buses get parked. As I stood talking to one of them, I noticed a wonderful game that several of the girls in the group directly across the hall from Danny's group were playing with their teachers' smiling consent.

One by one, they would run across the hallway and give Danny a pat on the head or a kiss on the cheek, then run back to their line, as the kids all up and down both lines would quietly squeal and giggle. Danny's teacher saw me watching and came over to fill me in.

"They love Danny because he is always laughing and waving his arms. But they know they have to be quick or he will grab them by the hair, so that's the trick. They started out just touching him on the arm, but then it was patting him on the head, then it was kissing his cheek. They love him so much."

That was a "wow" moment I have cherished and used during difficult, dark days over the past twenty-five years.

We celebrated Danny's fifth birthday and the fact that he had been completely seizure-free for several months. But the previous two years had left us whip-sawed from repeated periods of great promise and hope, followed by weeks of worry and fear for Danny's health, followed by more promise and hope. We had accepted that Danny would never be *normal*, that Angelman Syndrome would be the defining fact of Danny's life (and ours), and that life would never, ever again be what it was just five short years earlier.

By that time, I had changed sales jobs again, getting off the road in favor of a position that required me to make a ninety-mile drive to Atlanta each day, but enabled me to be home every night. We continued to struggle financially, as the house took most of whatever money I could earn, and the normal pressures of a competitive sales environment took a greater, and darker, toll on my energy and psyche.

It has been said that in times of great stress, we tend to fall back on old habits to get us through the day, and for me that meant a return to abusing alcohol on a daily basis. In sales, there is lots of unsupervised down time between appointments, and I spent much of that time with one of my fellow salesmen, drinking in the basement of his home, away from his hectoring wife and my stress-filled home life.

For the better part of three years, almost since our arrival in Georgia, my wife and I had developed clear lines of responsibility when it came to family life. I worked as hard and long as I could while she took care of Danny's treatment, Chrissy's normal childhood development and the home renovations. Although I had no love for sales, my communications background made me successful enough in it to provide a decent life for my family—almost. Money was always an issue, but that just meant our lives weren't completely different from most of the "normal" families we knew.

Fortunately, for all of us, it was at this time that Danny entered the public school system. Because he was handicapped, he was eligible to attend school beginning at age 5. That was a true Godsend for all of us, including our four-year-old daughter. Both are out of the public school system now (Danny aged out on his twenty-second birthday), and I can't think of any more positive experience in Danny's life than the wonderful teachers, aides and fellow students (both in his special needs classes and those in regular classes) that he encountered each day.

For parents of special needs kids, the sense of isolation and "apartness" can be overwhelming at times. Even your closest friends and family may have difficulty knowing what to say and do around your child, and their kids are often caught in the middle of an uncomfortable kabuki dance of proper behavior with and around your child's special needs.

School is the perfect opportunity for your special child to encounter "normal" on his or her own terms. Special needs parents can be the worst of the helicopter variety, constantly hovering over their child so that no one hurts or mistreats them, and so their child doesn't hurt or mistreat someone else. Any parent of a new first-grader can attest to the stress and worry of sending their little darling into the cold unknown world of school for the first time, and for the parent of the special needs child, the worry is exponentially worse.

But can I offer some encouragement from the advantage of nearly twenty years of 20/20 hindsight? School is a wonderful thing. Are all their teachers and aides going to be kind, caring and knowledgeable? Absolutely not; although I find that the vast majority of bad ones don't last more than one year.

Are there going to be stereotypical mean kids, taunting your child on the bus or in the hallway? Of course. But here's the thing, as pointed out to me by the parent of a teenager with seriously advanced cerebral palsy years before I was cast into the handicapped child world: your special needs child doesn't understand that he or she is being made fun of; he just knows people are giving him some attention and everyone is laughing. It may be cruel and unacceptable behavior to witness (and should never be tolerated or ignored), but the reality is your child is probably going to come away from the incident emotionally unscathed.

Are there going to be disagreements between you and the school over the services and care your child is receiving? Probably. But my experience is that the laws protecting special needs students and providing for their intellectual, social and physical development are quite clear and extensive, so the law is on your side. In fact, some of the requirements seem downright ridiculous to me, but they always err on offering your child the "most" from his or her school experience, not the least.

Of all the professionals I have encountered in my journey with Danny—doctors, therapists, nurses, medical specialists, case managers, researchers, public health officials—none come even close to the positive impact his teachers have had on his (and my) life. The love, laughter and acceptance Danny found in those elementary school hallways, and in his classrooms surrounded by other special needs kids and the teachers, aides and student helpers he encountered, left a lifelong impression on him—and me.

But of equal importance is the impression he had on them. I can't tell you how many young people I have encountered in Walmart, or on a job site, or in a restaurant who asked me about Danny. They had gone to school with him years before, but they remembered him. And they always said that with a big smile on their face, because I am quite certain they have some funny memory of him making a lot of noise in the high school hallway or in the pep rally, or throwing his food in the cafeteria, or just being his ornery self.

We are all created for a reason, in a place and a time chosen by God. I have worked for many years in volunteer ministry trying to impact others with the love and joy of God, but I am quite sure Danny has reached thousands more just by being Danny. Your special needs child needs school. More importantly, the world, kids in particular, need your special needs child in their lives.

One final word about school. My first career out of college was public school teacher, so I have seen this world from both sides of the desk. If you want your child to get the most out of his or her eighteen years in the school system, approach it as the most important partnership in your child's life. Only a very few teachers are in the business for any other reason than a love for children. Once upon a time, special needs teachers were often those who couldn't hack it any more in regular classrooms and were sent to babysit the handicapped kids until their retirement age finally rolled around.

I only encountered that with one teacher (and that teacher didn't even make it through the year). Special needs education is a very highly monitored area these days. In fact, many state legislatures have passed laws requiring cameras in all special needs classrooms to make sure the students aren't being abused by teachers or aides.

If you, as a parent, will approach your child's teacher assuming that you are dealing with a caring, trained, competent professional who is trying to balance your child's needs with the needs of a dozen other special needs students and a mountain of bureaucratic requirements and red tape, I think you will find a wonderful new key member to your child's care team.

Oh, and taking chocolate candy to your child's ARD meetings is a great icebreaker.

At the same time that we sent Danny off to public school, we enrolled his little sister into a wonderful day-care academy. Even though having Danny out of the house each day freed up a lot of my wife's time and energy, we felt it was imperative to give Chrissy a chance to be around normal, verbal kids. Because of Danny's lack of speech, Chrissy's own speech was significantly delayed, as were her social skills.

I can't stress this point enough. Your child may have the handicap, but the problem affects everyone in the household. It changes the family dynamic in ways that you won't even realize until years later (if ever). It is normal behavior to focus on the neediest members of your family, but that doesn't mean other family members' needs aren't real and ongoing.

Sadly, our family would soon learn this devastating and tragic fact of life.

Chapter 10
RETURN TO "NORMAL" LIFE

"For everything there is a season, and a time for every matter under heaven; a time to be born, and a time to die."
– Ecclesiastes 3:1-2

*T*rial and tragedy have a definite rhythm and cycle. At first, there is chaos, confusion and fear. Whether it is a medical crisis, job loss, marital split or act of God, your first task is to figure out where you are, what's really going on, and what needs to be done ***immediately***.

I remember telling a dear friend who had just discovered that her two infant daughters were afflicted with cystic fibrosis that one day life *would* return to normal. "It won't be the normal you've known all your life up to now, but there will be a new normal that you will wake up in someday."

During that first, chaotic period of crisis, though, everything changes all at once. Those projects you were pursuing at work cease to matter. Your friends' drama fades into the distance. In truth, real friends will stop talking about their needs and focus on your issues; bad friends will either quit talking to you completely or they will blather on and your overworked mind will quit listening.

Suddenly, family will be all that matters. That can be your blood family, or in many cases it will be your church family or your family of long-time, close friends. I define family as those people in your life that truly hurt when you hurt and are there whatever the need and whatever the inconvenient hour to walk with you through your desert experience.

In reality, though, life marches on for everyone. Our creditors didn't care that my wife and I were spending every bit of our time, energy and money on Danny's issues. There was a mortgage to be paid—and credit card bills, and car payments, and taxes. We had a small marketing business, and our customers still had needs and deadlines to be met.

As a parent of a child with any kind of long-term health or developmental need, you will eventually have to face the fact that you have entered into a lifetime of fence-straddling, caught between caring for your child and maintaining the rest of your family's financial, emotional, physical and spiritual life.

The hard truth is that your child will either not make it (which will lead to a whole host of other issues that I am not qualified to address), or your child will live and your family will make the necessary adjustments to deal with this new normal. This chaos, confusion and fear will slowly dissolve into determination and dedication. Your family and friends will go back to their lives, and eventually you will find yourself discussing mundane issues like homework, friends' marital problems and home repair projects.

That doesn't mean your life won't revolve around doctors' appointments, therapy sessions and the latest research on your child's affliction. Those will probably always be your front burner issues, but these are in addition to your old normal, not instead of it.

By the time you reach this stage, you also will have gotten over the shock that your child's life isn't going to be normal and that most of the dreams you've had for your child's future will never come to pass. You have adjusted your expectations. Instead of imagining your life as the proud parent of a star athlete, prima ballerina, life-saving doctor or political power broker, you dream of seeing your child take that first step, learn to use the toilet, sit up unassisted or just speak.

These realities take time to digest and accept, and in our case, most had solidified by the time Danny celebrated his sixth birthday and nearly three years of seizure-free existence. We still had hopes for some new cure for Danny's condition, but we were resigned to the fact that he would always be about eighteen months old, developmentally. At least he was physically healthy and was on a fairly low dose of medication to stave off breakthrough seizures.

Now that he was in the school system, he had an active social life, including spending large amounts of time away from his mom and me. He not only attended school every day, but he rode the school bus, giving him a completely new and exciting experience in seeing the world rolling by through large windows. He received therapy at school, plus he had water therapy a couple of days a week.

Water therapy was where he took his first steps. His inability to walk wasn't a muscle issue. It was a matter of balance, and the buoyancy of the water, plus the spatial cognition his upper body had with the surface of the water gave him the ability and confidence to step ever so slowly away from his handler and out on his own. One of the teachings at the Institute that we held tightly to was that development comes in small steps (figuratively and literally) and helps spur development in other areas of the brain.

With Chrissy also in a daycare academy to help with her speech and socialization skills, our family seemed to have finally found its new normal. That allowed us to turn back to the other family needs. Like how much money we needed but didn't have. And how much work our old house still needed. And how our social and church lives had become almost nonexistent.

For six years, I had been the primary fence-straddler for our family, as the kids' mom focused her time on meeting Danny's many needs, researching treatment options, tending to Chrissy's development and overseeing the major home renovation that seemed to go on forever.

With Danny and Chrissy happily ensconced into their daily schedules, she finally had options. She could work, too, and help bring in some much-needed household income. With her professional background, she might even be able to make enough money to replace me as the provider for the family and allow me to take the lead role in parenting. That idea appealed to both of us, as I was as burned out on trying to make ends meet as she was in trying to hold those ends together.

We made a deal. I wasn't happy with my job at the time, so both of us would put our resumes out wherever we could, and the one who got the best offer would take it. The other one would assume the bulk of the parenting duties and find whatever work that would help the budget without sacrificing too much time for Danny and Chrissy.

It sounded like a good, reasonable and highly doable plan.

Having survived six years of chaos, confusion and fear, it felt good to have what seemed to be a proactive plan for our lives again. No more chasing windmills. No more running around the country in search of the perfect program to fix Danny. No more major life moves. We would tackle the big problems in our lives one small bite at a time.

But the reality—the bitter, ugly truth—was that during all that time looking for answers to Danny's problem and making all those necessary adjustments, we had completely ignored the biggest challenges facing our family. We had not taken care of ourselves and each other.

As the parent of a special needs child, I can speak with great authority on a wide range of topics about the realities that you will face. I have seen the bad, and the good. And except for the death of a child, I think the worst possible outcome is the death of a family.

I believe that God will never give us more than we can bear—with His help. The problem is, we often get so caught up in the battle that we forget that we aren't in it alone. We try to fight it on our own power, and when we get our butts kicked, the worst parts of our personalities come to the fore. We resort to old habits and trust too much in old ways of thinking.

There is a rhythm and there are cycles to the trials and tragedies in our lives. Good times turn to bad times which turn to good times which eventually give way to...well, you get the idea. It is in those transitions that families get out of sync, schisms form and grow, opportunities are presented (and missed).

This is true for everyone's life. But when you have a special needs child, the valleys can be terribly deep, which make the high points seem epically high. We need someone to cling to, to reassure us, to really listen and not offer judgments or fixes. Just listen. As a couple, we're on the same roller coaster, but not necessarily in the same car, moving at the same speed or even at the same spot on the track.

In retrospect, it is amazing how blind we both were to what was really happening. Our daughter was struggling with her speech because she lived in constant and close proximity with a brother who had no speech but for whom special considerations were made to work around that. She also struggled socially because we didn't have a wide range of friends with children in our lives anymore. It was so much easier to just stay home and avoid places and activities where Danny's handicap might cause disruption.

Since I had spent several years traveling all week to my job assignments out of town, and now worked a job that required me to make many after-hours sales calls a couple of hours away from home, the weekends were generally reserved for catching up on the work that I needed to do around the house, or the hard discussions and arguments that my wife and I needed to have about bills and day-to-day problems.

I was up and out of the house every morning before the kids were even awake, and often didn't get home until long after their bedtimes. Another hard truth is that by the time I got home, I was too inebriated to interact with them in a positive way.

My wife was bored out of her mind, and desperately in need of a break from this monotony. We had prayed for things to calm down just a couple of years earlier, when we were in the crisis of the seizure years. But that was then; this was now. There were no pressing medical issues to deal with or research to be done. Doing the program was far, far in the past; besides, most of the work on Danny was being done at school and by his therapist.

I slipped further and further into the black hole of depression and alcoholism. The estrangement my family had felt with the world ever since we left Texas intertwined with the low self-esteem and high self-doubt I had felt since I was a child. Work was an unending nightmare of missed quotas, angry lectures from our demanding boss and frustration with unsuccessful sales appointments. There was no relief at work or at home, except in the bottle of vodka that was always at my side during the two-hour trips back and forth to Atlanta and during the long waits between sales calls.

My wife and I are both intelligent, aware people who love our kids dearly and would do anything for them. Except pay attention and be brutally honest with one another.

They say what doesn't kill you makes you stronger. The problem is that sometimes in the midst of battle, you can't tell if you are growing— or dying.

We were dying and didn't even realize it.

Chapter 11
THE END OF THE RIDE

"I have before you life and death, blessing and curse. Therefore, choose life, that you and your offspring may live, loving the Lord your God, obeying His voice and holding fast to him."
– Deuteronomy 30:19-20

T he fourth stage of grieving, as defined by Elisabeth Kubler-Ross, is depression. This follows the denial, anger and bargaining stages. You can no longer deny the reality of the grief-causing event, and you have exhausted all the tears and rage your body and soul can manage. You have accepted that there is no deal to be made with God or the devil that will change anything.

It is quite possible to find yourself left with nothing but sadness, loneliness and depression about the dreams left behind and the hard reality ahead. It is, as they say, what it is. You are on the hard road of your reality, and it has become a well-marked trail of broken dreams, dashed hopes, seemingly unanswered prayers and failed "fixes."

Danny's handicap completely and immediately altered the path of our entire family and every member of it. We moved halfway across the country. We abandoned friends and business and church. We gave up whatever dreams we had carried with us since childhood and focused completely on dealing with his issues. Nothing else mattered. Certainly not career or finances. All our future plans centered around how we were going to fix Danny and, once that was done, we could figure the rest of it out.

But reality doesn't always turn out the way we hope. In fact, it rarely does. Despite all the money, effort, tears and time we devoted to the goal, Danny reached a certain level of development, and there he stayed. In fact, he is still there. (As I write this, we are sitting on our back screened-in patio and Danny is sitting in his rocking chair laughing maniacally at something he sees or perceives in the back yard. I can't see anything except the softness of the green grass and shrubs in the coming dusk, and the cicadas are drowning out any other sounds, so who knows what this laughter is all about? But Danny is happy, so who cares?)

After all the big changes, the disappointments, the anger and finally accepting Danny for who he is, we were basically back to square one, redefining our lives and our marriage in light of all this new information. And we had to do it as two deeply burdened souls searching for meaning and direction without the benefit of a solid, healthy support team holding us up during the battle.

When all else has failed, where do you turn? That would be the question that defined, and transformed, the next stage of our family's life. And in hindsight, we did what most people do in times of crisis: we returned to our roots.

I was raised on a small dairy farm in Texas. There were many wonderful things I experienced and learned through farm life, but it wasn't until I was in my mid-forties and facing life with a handicapped child that I realized the value of dealing with monotony and never-ending responsibility for another being. I remember how I celebrated when my dad sold the farm and retired when I was a high school sophomore; finally, I would have a chance to escape this drudgery and enjoy all the exotic, fun opportunities the non-farm world had to offer.

And I had spent most of my adult life chasing new experiences. I quickly ditched my chosen career as a school teacher for the chance to meet new people and write about their lives, first as a sports writer, then as a feature writer and editor. I interviewed business leaders, fashion designers, musicians, politicians, even people living off the grid in tarpaper huts and dug-out ditches on government lands. I changed jobs every couple of years as I climbed journalism's corporate ladder, excited about each new challenge, but soon found that they too contained the same old politics, routines and (horror of horrors) monotony that every other career move eventually revealed.

When I met my kids' mom, her nomadic past appealed greatly to my need to escape the dead-end corporate world I kept falling into. As a child, her family had lived all over the country, never putting down roots anywhere (contrasted with my life in the same house from the time I was two until I left home for college).

Within months of meeting, we had both abandoned our previous lives (including marriages and career paths) and embarked on a new dream of running a small marketing business that would free us up and give us opportunity to travel and spend lots of time with our church family.

I also left behind a big part of my old life—excessive drinking to cope with the stress of my life as a writer and manager of a small magazine. Drinking had been a tool I had used to deal with pain and loneliness, and to give me confidence and boldness, through my many life and career changes since high school days.

I seriously cut back on the drinking when I first met my kids' mom and stopped completely once we discovered she was pregnant. I was in a state of nirvana and no chemical assistance was needed. I stayed that way through the birth of my daughter. But when we moved to Georgia and I took a job that required me to travel out of town for days at a time, the loneliness of the road and the lack of accountability to anyone caught up with me and I slowly slipped back into the old habits.

By Danny's sixth birthday, I was working in a very high stress sales environment and drinking after work was just part of the routine (our boss would buy the first round, no matter how angry he was with us for missing our weekly sales quotas).

This is not meant to be an excuse for my bad behavior. I was old enough to know better and I knew my history with alcohol. I also knew the challenges that faced me at home, and I found it easier to grab a few rounds at the bar than to just say no and head back into the same-old challenges of finances, Danny's struggles, Chrissy's temper tantrums and my wife's growing disenchantment with the whole monotonous mess.

Her old coping mechanism wasn't found in a bottle. It was in new challenges, new places, new people, new adventures. While I struggled to face another sales pitch, she battled the boredom of spending another day with one nonverbal child, one needy toddler, a pile of unpaid bills and a level of monotony that she had never experienced.

In short, I settled back into an old habit that brought instant relief, and she set her sights on something different. It took another couple of years, and there was lots of bickering and promises to do better and attempts to try to find common ground, and even a couple of big life changes. I changed sales jobs, we sold our remodeled home, and moved closer to Atlanta to cut down on commuting times and give the kids' mom a better chance to find work outside the home.

There were lots of cosmetic changes to our rotting marriage, but the inner damage was so deep that neither of us seemed to see or understand exactly what was happening and, more importantly, what it would take to stop the decline. I had grown up thinking I was a failure and this reality I was living seemed to affirm that, at home and at work. My wife grew up as a fighter and an overcomer, and her inability to defeat this "Danny problem" left her with a yearning to go somewhere else and do something where she could win again.

By this time, Danny had become almost an afterthought. His care was left mostly to his teachers at school, his therapists, and a very sweet teenage girl who watched him after school. My new job took me from home until late most nights and the kids' mom spent most of her time working in a job she hated and trying to figure out her next step to bring some joy back into her life.

Our new normal was a life of bills, work stress, the challenges of raising a preschooler, and the same old, same old life with Danny—changing diapers, feeding him, bathing him, taking him to therapy every week. Even with Chrissy, we were often relegated to taxi driver and appointment scheduler. She had her own set of issues, and we did what we thought was necessary, but the truth is that our home was a mortuary of broken dreams, stress and codependent coping skills. The adults in the house had become the real problem, unable to care for themselves or their kids.

We both knew it, deep down, in spite of the fact that neither of us wanted to admit defeat. But it was the reality. We had failed, and our failure had become the greatest threat to Danny—and Chrissy—and their development. The pain was numbing and searing, and we could not bear it together. There was just too much of it. Counseling only works if everyone involved is one the same page working toward the same goal. We had passed the point of no return.

We had hit the bottom of the last big hill of our roller-coaster ride as parents of a handicapped child. Now it was just a matter of slowly making our way back to the station and getting off the ride—in separate directions.

Chapter 12
A NEW CRISIS AND A NEW REALITY

"Even though I walk through the valley of the shadow of death, I will fear no evil, for you are with me; your rod and your staff, they comfort me."

— Psalm 23:4

I earnestly believe the scripture that says that God will never give us more than we can handle—with His help. But that doesn't mean we won't be tested—often beyond what we believe to be our limits. In fact, that's how we grow in our relationship with God. When we reach the end of our rope, we call out to God in desperation, and He gets us through the crisis of the moment. And if we are smart, we take note of that dynamic and stop waiting until all else fails to make that call.

In the midst of dealing with my personal emotional breakdown from seeing my marriage collapse, I suddenly was jolted back to the reality that I had a special needs child to care for, and that my needs were going to have to move to the back burner for a while.

God has a funny way of putting things in perspective like that.

A couple of nights before New Year's 2001, as I was getting the kids ready for bed, Danny started throwing up. This was more annoying than alarming, as I had just bathed him and now I had to strip the bed, give him a sponge bath, put clothes and linens in the laundry, aerate the room and try not to lose my own dinner in the smelly process.

But there was no time to wallow in self-pity, as Danny did it again, and we started the whole process over. Only this time, he didn't stop. He continued to throw up. I yelled for my seven-year-old daughter to come out of her room and help me with the towels, since I couldn't leave Danny's side for fear he would lie back and aspirate some of the vomit.

After nearly an hour of fighting this battle, I grabbed the phone and called his pediatrician. By now, it was after 10:00 on a weekend night just before New Year's Eve, and I could tell when the doctor called me back that he was at a party and had been in the middle of having an enjoyable evening with friends (I vaguely recalled doing things like that myself in my younger, pre-parent days).

The doctor said he would call in a prescription for Phenergan, which would stop the vomiting and help Danny get to sleep. It wasn't until I went out to warm up the car that I realized that we were in the grips of a pretty substantial sleet storm. I had to take both kids with me, as Chrissy was far too young to be left alone at home. By now, Danny had thrown up everything in his stomach, so he was reduced to dry heaving and some intermittent bile.

Slowly we eased out of our steep driveway and made our way through the deserted white streets of Conyers, Georgia. When I got to the supermarket, I saw only a handful of people inside, so I parked my car directly in front of the main entry, ran in and grabbed a kid mopping the aisles. He was shocked (as was I at my boldness) when I dragged him to the front door and ordered him to stand watch over my kids in the idling car while I raced back to the pharmacy to pick up my prescription.

We made it back home and somehow got up the icy driveway. I carried Danny in, laid him on a pallet of towels in the living room and administered the first of several suppositories that I would dispense that night. I prayed they would work, and Danny's heaving would cease, and he would mercifully go to sleep. But God had another plan.

Two hours and several suppositories later, I called the doctor again, who by now had made it home and was not particularly happy about being woken up. He told me to give one more dose, but if that didn't stop the vomiting to take him to the hospital. "Call me tomorrow," he grumbled, which I took to mean, "Do not bother me again tonight."

Of course, the final dose of this anti-nausea medication didn't work, because the nausea wasn't the problem. We were in the middle of a major seizure episode—the worst I think we had seen since completing the Ketogenic diet. The nausea was merely a manifestation of the seizure, and the Phenergan did nothing for that.

That's what I know now, but all I knew for sure at the time was that I had a very sick kid and it was totally up to me to deal with it. There was no wife to turn to, no doctor's advice to follow. The reality of being a single dad had arrived with the full force of a January ice storm.

Although the local hospital was only ten minutes away, I knew they would not actually treat my special needs child. They would simply stabilize him and call for an ambulance to transport him to a larger hospital with specialists trained for his unique challenges. That would mean several wasted hours before we could get to the bottom of this crisis and get to the "real" treatment.

So once again I loaded the kids in the car, having packed blankets and other provisions just in case the worst happened and we slid off the icy road along the way, because the hospital we were headed for was on the far side of Atlanta—a forty-minute drive in good conditions. Chrissy immediately went to sleep in the back seat. I put Danny next to me so he could lay his head on my shoulder and sit upright, and I could quickly clean up anything his dry heaving produced.

I gathered the remaining supplies, locked the front door behind me, and came to a rude awakening, literally, about the dire conditions awaiting me on this trip. As I stepped down from our front porch, my feet flew out from under me and I found myself sliding quickly down our steep front yard. I frantically kicked the ice trying to gain a foothold, because the street below was equally steep and I knew if I was still sliding when I got there I wouldn't stop until I got all the way to the bottom of the hill, leaving me with a very treacherous and time-consuming climb back up to my kids. I began to panic and to cry out to God (or anyone who might be out taking a stroll at 1:00 a.m. in the ice) for immediate help.

Fortunately, my foot caught on the curb and I stopped. I crawled on hands and knees back up the hill, made it to the car, and climbed in for the next part of this insane adventure. At least all fears of being too sleepy to make the drive had been left in my front yard.

The drive to the hospital was equally maddening, as my heart and mind were already racing, but even the slightest pressure on the accelerator would send the rear of the car into a slow slide one way or the other, and stop signs had to be approached with the same caution one might take with a rattlesnake or a sleeping baby. Slowly, slowly, slowly we eased our way around I-285. I stopped counting the wrecks we passed at nineteen. The drive took more than ninety excruciating minutes.

Children's Medical Center was dark and deserted when we arrived, with only the lights of the Emergency Room beckoning through the sleet. The sense of relief I felt on having arrived safely was tempered by the eeriness of the dimly lit and abandoned lobby area. The staff got Danny on a gurney and hurried him through giant, forbidding doors while I made Chrissy a bed on a bench just outside the ER, got her settled and spoke briefly to a sleepy security guard about keeping an eye on her.

By the time I made it back to Danny's side, they had already gotten tubes through his nose and down into his stomach, started an IV and had him hooked up to a variety of monitors. Like most of the ER staffs I have encountered over the years, they were coolly efficient and professional, although their calmness in the midst of my crisis was a bit off-putting (I realize that is their training, but this is *my* kid and *my* crisis and I want them to understand just how critical this situation is).

I explained what had been happening for the past four hours and the steps I had taken, on doctor's orders, to address it. They said the nausea was probably the result of some bug going around, or something he ate, or some other simple explanation that they see all the time, and all we need to do is give him something to stop the vomiting. I agreed with their plan, since they are the experts, you know, and by now my body and mind were in full fatigue mode. Just let somebody else make the decision and get on with it.

A drug was administered through IV and we waited. At first the results looked promising, but soon he was back to dry heaving as violently as he had earlier in the evening. The doctor came back in, mumbled to himself as he examined Danny more closely, studied the chart, and stepped outside to confer with a nurse. I followed and finally got up the nerve to offer my two-cents worth—which was about the value they placed on it.

"I think this is a seizure. Maybe we should try some Diazepam." This was a drug we had gotten very familiar with during Danny's previous seizure episodes. It had never failed to immediately break the seizure.

The doctor was extremely skeptical and dismissive. No way this was a seizure, he said. He's vomiting and now he is dehydrated. Let's give this a little more time and see what happens.

Even though I had been out of the day-to-day loop in caring for Danny for several years, this was way too familiar of the early days when we had doctors dismissing our concerns that there was something seriously wrong with him, that he was just a "late bloomer."

We waited and we watched the nurses try to calm Danny during his dry heaving and his nonstop attempts to pull the tubes out of his nose and the IV out of his arm. Another hour passed, and finally, I had had enough. I demanded that they treat this as a seizure and that they administer the Diazepam. That, I was told, would have to be approved by the head ER doctor on duty at the time.

She was summoned. She was not in agreement but said they would do it if I agreed to sign some releases stating that this was what I wanted to do and that it was being done over their objections. The forms were signed, the drug was administered and within minutes the seizures stopped. The nightmare came to a merciful end.

As the sun came up and blazed off the sea of ice outside, Danny was admitted to a room, where he slept soundly. One of the neurologists on staff stopped by and I explained what had occurred the night before. He, too, was skeptical that the nausea was a seizure. "There's nothing in the literature to support that," he said.

"Then write this up and there will be something in the literature," I suggested, probably a little more sarcastically than I should have. They never were able to precisely diagnose what the source of the vomiting was, but they never agreed with me in person or in writing that this was a serious seizure episode. They were convinced it was a bug (which they were unable to detect) or something he had eaten (again, no evidence, just their working theory). But I know what I saw, and I believe what I believe.

I was encouraged to take my daughter and go home for a few hours of rest and a shower.

Chrissy was back asleep before we got out of the parking lot, and I wept all the way home as the worry, the fear, the exhaustion, the anger, and the reality of my new situation all settled in at once.

I was a single parent and I had just survived the first of many tests.

Chapter 13
HARD CHOICES

"We know that for those who love God all things work together for good, for those who are called according to His purposes."
– Romans 8:28

O n September 11, 2001, a bright, sunny morning along the East Coast turned into the darkest day in American history since the assassination era of the mid-1960s. Four airlines filled with innocent victims rained down on office buildings and a Pennsylvania field, stopping the whole world in its tracks. The horror was followed by rage followed by grief and fear of what would come next.

Like many Americans, that day shook me to my core, and at one point I could go no further with my sales routine. I pulled off the country road I was traveling, found a safe place to park, and sat in my truck and wept. Because this tragedy was just another land mine along the dark path I had been traveling since the beginning of that terrible year.

It started immediately after my experience with Danny's late-night seizures and the mad dash through the ice to Children's Hospital in Atlanta. My marriage was in full melt-down mode and there was absolutely nothing I could do about it. There had been months of shock and rage and accusations and visits to lawyers.

I could not believe this was happening. How could my family be dissolving right before my eyes? Where was the fix for this? The counselors we visited had no plan, except to help me adjust to life as a single parent. My friends and co-workers were equally shocked and kept assuring me this would eventually blow over if I just gave it time.

But in my heart, I knew better. I had already been down this road with Danny's diagnosis, and I had learned to trust my gut. And my gut, when it stopped churning with sickening heartbreak, told me to get a grip and start making some hard decisions for Danny and Chrissy. And myself—because it was all up to me.

Here I was, thrust unwillingly onto uncharted waters of raising a handicapped child, without the support, counsel, and bravery, of my copilot for the past ten years. I read every book I could find to prepare me and help me make the right decisions; I talked to everyone I knew (and a few I didn't know at all), I counseled with my pastor. I wept uncontrollably. I drank heavily. When all else failed, I prayed.

I had spent weeks swinging from deep depression to wild rage as I battled with the pain and anger constantly boiling within me. My sleep had gotten erratic at best, and my drinking was bordering on being completely out of control. All this stress and emotional devastation resulted in me developing serious back problems, and there was no position I could find in standing, sitting or even lying down that didn't send sharp pains up and down my spine and legs.

A doctor at a walk-in clinic prescribed some mild pain medication for me, but that just made me groggy at a time when I needed to have my wits about me more than ever, as I struggled to do my demanding job, take care of the kids and fight with my soon-to-be ex-wife.

Finally, God responded to my never-ending cries for guidance. One stormy spring afternoon, the pain in my back made thinking, much less speaking, a soul-sucking challenge, so I had finally given up, cancelled my last two sales appointments, and suffered the hour-long drive home in Atlanta traffic.

As I pulled into my driveway, the rain turned to a deluge. I sat in my truck for about five minutes waiting for it to ease up, but it just seemed to get harder. I dreaded getting soaked, but my back was screaming for some type of relief. Summoning up all my courage and strength, I flung the door open and leapt from the seat, hoping that I would be able to finish the eight steps to the garage before my back realized the assault it was under.

But the moment my feet hit the ground and I tried to stand up, my back and legs went into total revolt mode, and simply gave way. I fell in a heap on the flooded driveway, my glasses going one way and my cellphone the other. As I lay there feeling the puddles around me to find my lost items, I finally just gave up and did what I should have done years before. "OK, God," I said. "You have my full, undivided attention now. What do you want from me?" I just laid my shoulder down on the concrete drive, struggling to keep my head above the puddle and ignoring the fact that within the past thirty seconds every inch of my body had become soaked in rainwater.

God replied: "Get up." It was a simple answer, but one God has been using for thousands of years. He told Abraham to get up and go— don't worry about where, I'll show you. He told Moses to get up and go get his fellow Jews out of slavery. He even told Joseph to get up and take Mary, who was pregnant with the Lord Jesus at the time, to Jerusalem for the census so that all prophecy regarding the Messiah's coming could be fulfilled.

And I laughed in disbelief and defiance. "Get up? That's it? That's all you've got for me now? I'm pretty sure you know what's been going on in my life lately. For months I've been drowning emotionally and financially and spiritually, and all you have to offer is 'Get up?'"

Eighteen years have passed since I lay in my driveway in the rain, and God has ordered me to "Get up" several more times, and as much as I fought it every time, those were the first hard steps to a better life that He had in store for me. God wants to lead us into paths of righteousness, but we have to be willing to stand up and step out in faith.

So I got up, crawled into the house and began making plans to move back to Texas—to family, friends, familiar places, and the support system I would need to make this work.

Even though I believed this was God's will, I knew it wasn't going to be easy. We arrived back in Texas with no money, no home and a new job in a field that I knew very little about.

Looking back on it, this also was the point in my life where Danny became just one more member of the family. There were no therapy sessions or special programs to contend with. Life was about finding summer care and after school care for both him and Chrissy (a real challenge since no daycare in the area would accommodate a special needs child), training new doctors about Danny's needs, and locating a place of our own to live while we boarded temporarily with my brother and sister.

And there was the small matter of my own broken, angry and despondent heart to overcome. I put on a good front of making it all about the kids, but inside I was barely holding it together. I was drinking a lot and swinging wildly between deep depression and wild fits of rage. My oldest brother, Doug, literally carried me through this period, babysitting the kids while I was at work, and babysitting me late at night as I sat in his room drinking beer and pouring out my heart.

This was my new normal. Danny was just another piece in a really hard puzzle. By now, I knew Danny's daily routine so well I could do it half asleep (or half-drunk as was often the case). I knew the signs to watch for that would indicate health issues and potential seizure relapses. I knew how to talk to school administrators, teachers, aides, therapists, counselors and doctors. The nine years of experience I had with Danny's issues and the rarity of Angelman Syndrome put me way ahead of them when it came to discussing his care.

Sadly, the fact that I, a man, was raising my kids (especially a handicapped kid) made me something of an oddity and a marvel. These professionals usually dealt with moms. I was never comfortable with the accolades this fact often brought. I saw it as a sad statement on my gender as a whole.

God certainly did His part. I found a job as a salesman for a lumber yard, for which I really wasn't qualified. But it came with a wonderful boss who gave me lots of grace and encouragement, both with learning how to do it, and making it work with my family responsibilities. Within weeks of returning to Texas, I found a place where I could not only live, but actually purchase (in spite of being in the midst of a bankruptcy at the time). It belonged to a dear friend from my past who not only would play a huge role at that critical point in my life but would eventually be an integral part of my family's future. I never cease to be amazed at how God uses people from our past to answer our prayers, bringing them back into our lives at the moment when we have given up hope.

In so many ways, my life was incredibly blessed. I still ached for all that I had lost, I still drank too much to staunch the pain, but I truly believed we were living in God's provision and that He really would provide for all my needs.

But once again I soon stopped listening to God and started paying more attention to my own, booze-addled ego. With a job and a place to live resolved, I turned my attention to finding after-school care for the kids. I was referred to a daycare for special needs kids who might also take in Danny's sister. The lady who ran it was a nurse and she had a handicapped child of her own, which prevented her from working a regular job, so she did this to earn money while tending to his needs.

From the moment I met her, I thought, "God, you are GOOD. This is perfect." She loved Danny AND Chrissy on sight. She had been in the process of adopting her son when it was determined the drug use by his biological mother had left him with very severe mental and physical handicaps, so the adoption process was set aside and she became his caretaker (just one of the many odd and unfortunate realities of how the handicapped world conflicts with legal issues and governmental programs supposedly designed to help those who can't help themselves).

In addition to meeting my immediate needs, this person's life helped put my own struggles into perspective. My son might be nonverbal; hers screamed for hours on end. Danny couldn't walk, but was able to crawl anywhere he wanted to go, often at a speed that challenged my abilities to keep up and intervene before he got somewhere he shouldn't be. Her son was confined to a bed 24/7 and had to be physically lifted out and cared for daily to prevent bedsores.

For months, I was able to relax a bit and let the new team member take a lead, not only in meeting Danny's daily needs, but in Chrissy's too. That allowed me to focus on learning my job and tending to my broken heart. But as often happens, when we get through our crises and life's cycles smooth out again, we take our eyes off God and return to old thought habits. And making the same old mistakes that had plagued me my whole life.

Within months, my caretaker's life took some difficult turns and we found ourselves in a relationship that I don't think God had in mind when I added her to my support team. Deep in my heart, I knew this was a bad idea. I knew getting involved with someone so quickly after we both had gone through divorce was very ill-advised. But my bruised ego turned my eyes from the real prize and to more base desires.

Because at that moment, it wasn't about Danny or Chrissy. Oh, I could give lots of good reasons for this being the best choice at the time. She had a handicapped child and understood what those realities are like; she deeply wanted a daughter and I deeply wanted Chrissy to have a full-time mom so I didn't have to figure out how to raise her on my own; she respected the hard choices I had made over the past few months, and I desperately needed that affirmation to do what needed to be done.

In short order, everything that they say about getting involved on the rebound came true, as we discovered that there were many things about each other's personalities that we didn't like. It just didn't work out, and in less than two years I ended up moving back to life as a single parent, more broken, discouraged and depressed than ever.

But that experience did teach me a few things about the handicapped world. First, until you have walked in the shoes of the parent or caregiver of a severely handicapped child, you really have no idea what their life is like, so keep your judgments to yourself. I had been in that world for nine years, but the challenge of caring for a bedridden, tube-fed, constantly screaming but very sweet young boy was harder than I ever imagined.

I developed a whole new level of gratitude for Danny's level of *involvement*, as I would watch this other poor child wracked by whatever inner physical turmoil left him in such misery. I stood in awe of the love and dedication his mom (a.k.a., caretaker) showed as she would rock him and soothe him, despite being totally exhausted and frustrated by the situation.

In the end, it was a short interlude in my family's strange journey, but it definitely had lasting effects on me and my daughter, in both positive and negative ways.

The most positive effect was that just before it all came crashing down, through one of my soon-to-be ex-wife's relatives, my daughter found her way to God, and drug me along with her.

Chapter 19
LONELINESS AND BAD CHOICES

"Fear not, stand firm, and see the salvation of the Lord, which He will work for you today... The Lord will fight for you, and you only have to be silent."

– Exodus 14:13-14

As I write this chapter, it is Father's Day. I am sitting in the bedroom I share with Danny. I just finished feeding him lunch, and he is watching *Wall-E* and whining because I am not giving him my undivided attention since I am busy writing. We are 16 years past the events of the previous chapter, and I am still battling the loneliness and despondency that led me to make so many bad, harmful decisions back when this Texas journey began.

Ultimately, the real problem we have had to confront throughout all those bad years wasn't Danny's developmental delays and occasional medical issues. Those are just the facts of who he is—no different from my being left-handed or my daughter having natural brown hair, which she occasionally changes to blonde or, for a while, a nice shade of purple.

The real problem that my family had to overcome throughout all this was my battle with depression and the questionable decisions I was prone to make because of that. To quote the great philosopher Pogo, "We have met the enemy and it is us."

Having a child means you, as an adult, get to choose how you work out your own issues in life while simultaneously teaching the next generation how they should face life when it is their turn. We all make mistakes. We all have regrets. And we all have sleepless nights of dread and worry when our children leave the nest and strike out on their own.

Only, with a handicapped child, chances are they never leave. They change and adapt, just like any other child. But the responsibility for meeting their daily needs remains. We hire workers to help us; sometimes we find homes where they can be placed on a permanent basis. But for many of the parents I know (and I know some who are in their eighties, caring for offspring in their sixties), the choice to care for their own child is a lifelong commitment.

Some call that heroic. Some call it foolish and even selfish. I call it following your heart, whatever that is. Each decision brings its own rewards and challenges. I can only address what I know, so I will focus on the choice to be the primary care provider for your handicapped child until death do you part.

When the dust settled on my unfortunate and sad attempt at trying to replace the kids' mom with someone I barely knew, I found myself back in the same place I had been in (at least emotionally and financially) when I first returned to Texas. As a one-income household, I struggled to make ends meet, working long hours (which meant paying overtime to my teen-age after-school caregiver) and arriving home exhausted and frazzled.

Life became a day-to-day survival, with no time or money for any "extra" treatment for Danny. He got physical and speech therapy at school, and seemed happy and content with his teachers, therapists, baby-sitters and even the grumpy bus driver. But that is the beauty of Angelman Syndrome—happiness and excitability are two of its main characteristics. In fact, before an English doctor by the name of Angelman identified the precise chromosomal defect and gave it his name in 1964, Angelman persons were often described as having "Happy Puppet Syndrome," since they are prone to laughing wildly and waving their arms up and down.

Danny had found his normal. I was still struggling with mine—and worrying incessantly about Chrissy's. Shy by nature, she was having a hard time fitting in at school, and the emotional roller coaster of the previous two years losing her biological mom, then having a "replacement mom" thrust into her life, then losing that person, had left her with a flat affect and few friends at school.

I was losing the battle with loneliness and depression, with alcohol as my primary weapon of defense. The weeks were blurs of long hard days at work, fighting with Chrissy to make sure she got her school work done, talking on the phone with her teachers and counselors as we tried to help her break out of her solemn shell, and the usual nightly routine of feeding, cleaning and getting everyone to bed, hopefully with enough time and energy left to sit on the porch and sip on a cold one.

It seemed like a beating at the time. But all these years later, I realize how God works His wonders even when we don't see it. And He does it in the most amazing ways. Because throughout all these difficult times there was one constant that held us together—Danny. No matter how dire the finances looked, or how lonely I felt, or how sad or angry Chrissy seemed, Danny was Danny.

When God spoke those immortal words of hope recorded in Jeremiah 29:11, He knew His plans for Israel and that they were for them to prosper and have hope and a future. But when you look at the context of this scripture, it was given to a group of people living in exile as a result of their disobedience to God. The people were calling out for deliverance and restoration to their homeland, but four verses before God gave them this promise He gave them an order: "seek the peace and prosperity of the city to which I have carried you into exile. Pray to the Lord for it, because if it prospers, you too will prosper."

In other words, don't ask for God to remove the challenges before you. He wouldn't remove the thorn in Paul's side or prevent Joseph from being sold into slavery or put into prison. He wouldn't even remove the bitter cup of crucifixion from His own son's painful last days. He not only asked them to accept these mountains, but to give thanks for them. Because it is through our struggles that we draw closest to Him and bring glory to Him.

Danny's problems had a direct impact on my life and the life of my daughter, and eventually both of us came to see that that impact was far more positive than negative. It shaped our thinking and became the backdrop of all our hopes and dreams. It was that constancy and responsibility of dealing with Danny that pulled me back from the edge of other bad decisions many times. It also gave me a greater sense of purpose. This was our normal and even if it wasn't great much of the time, it was ours all the time. I learned years later that Chrissy felt those same determined feelings, even at her young age. Just as being "Danny's dad" gave me my identity and raison d'etre, having a mentally handicapped brother provided the same direction for her.

And God kept showing up right in the middle of my mess in many different places and forms. Toward the end of my failed marriage to the nurse with the handicapped child, Chrissy had visited a church with a friend, and for the first time ever she came home demanding that I take her back. That church, and the loving people we encountered there, helped us both through some very dark days. It was a church that was all about having a personal relationship with Jesus Christ, and that literally changed all our lives.

That doesn't mean all our problems were solved and we all lived happily ever after. Both my daughter and I continue to battle the demons of depression, but we do so knowing that there is hope. We have better weapons to use. We have encouraging friends affirming us and lifting us up in prayer. We have a chance to serve others who are struggling with their own issues, helping keep ours in perspective.

Caring for a handicapped child can put you into a totally separate and isolated world. Your child doesn't behave the way others do, often refusing to sit still and be quiet in public places like church, school events and movies. Visiting friends in their homes can be a challenge since your child may have to be constantly watched lest they do damage to property or other children. Even family gatherings in your own home can be a problem, as your nonverbal but loud child can be a damper on conversation.

You find yourself turning down invitations, staying at home, sitting on the porch away from the crowd inside, or arriving late and leaving early. Life is easiest in a controlled environment, which often means a safe room in your own home. Danny seems to have adjusted to the isolation pretty well, rarely demanding attention—except when I am around and he thinks I am giving too much of it to someone or something else.

If I seem to be dwelling on this loneliness issue too much, I offer no apologies. It has been my greatest struggle and it is a common theme I hear expressed by the parents of other handicapped individuals I know. They usually express it as a frustration with the lack of available activities for their children, but I see it in their eyes. Yes, they want the best for their kids. But they also are looking to fill the hole left in their lives with their decision to choose this over what the rest of the world is experiencing, which we all see being detailed in daily Facebook posts and Instagram photos.

There are many great programs for handicapped children and adults, even in the small Texas community where I resided for most of my time raising Danny. We are all thankful for those programs and the wonderful, caring people behind them. But those are momentary distractions from weeks and months of the daily grind of feeding, diapering, dressing and playing God for our charges.

I envy those functional families who have both parents, and grandparents, and aunts, uncles, cousins and loving friends who join in this unique journey. Unfortunately, I see a lot of single moms, a few single dads and a good number of aging grandparents who have picked up the banner to fight the good fight on behalf of someone who can't. I have been blessed with people around me who care about Danny's welfare and mine; some from my natural and married family, some from my church family, some just because they know Danny from somewhere over the years.

At the end of the day, I know I am blessed. God truly has used this journey to teach me about His love and His provision. Danny's normal may not be what most would call "normal," but in many ways it is better. He is surrounded by people who love him and constantly watch over him; he has no real worries; he never misses a meal, a comfortable place to sleep or a rapid response to a dirty diaper.

Then again, neither do I. God has this. He always has and He always will. I just need to not let myself get distracted from the truth.

But knowing a truth and following it are two different things entirely. I may know the truth, but the days can be long and hard, and the lonely nights can be even more so. And old habits are hard to break.

Chapter 15
WHAT "NORMAL" LOOKS LIKE

"Get wisdom; get insight; do not forget, and do not turn away from the words of my mouth. Do not forsake her, and she will keep you; love her, and she will guard you."

– Proverbs 4:5-6

I t is pouring rain—so hard that the narrow, winding, pothole-filled road ahead of me is almost impassable. Any speed over twenty mph is sheer lunacy or foolish teenage bravado, as evidenced by the carful that just passed around me going up a steep hill that totally blocked their view of oncoming traffic.

Still, their honking and middle-finger waving have no effect on me as I plod along, as focused as possible on the hazards ahead. To my right, Danny is as frustrated as those impatient teens. He is banging on the ceiling of my pickup, whining loudly and kicking the floorboard. He loves riding in the truck, but he hates going slow.

You want to know what raising a handicapped child is *really* like? How are my parental challenges different from those parents with "normal" kids? This is it. Yes, there are the occasional terror-filled evenings of uncontrollable seizures, the soul-crushing telephone conversations with uninformed and unsympathetic government bureaucrats over the level of service they will pay for, the sleepless nights of worry about some decision you have made on your child's behalf that could possibly affect his quality of life forever.

But for the most part, daily life with a handicapped child is learning to live with their needs and idiosyncrasies. That means not being unnerved or angry when your child does something like banging his hands and arms on the ceiling of the car when traffic comes to a halt. It means always keeping an eye on your child's sippy cup as it can become a dangerous flying projectile the moment he finishes the contents inside or just gets bored with it. It means always checking around your vehicle for items that the child may have tossed out the window while you were loading groceries or pumping gas.

Danny needs assistance with walking, and he is not above just sitting down wherever he happens to be when he decides that he has done enough walking for the day. That can be in the middle of a busy hallway at a medical clinic, or the middle of a parking lot. You have to know your child and his or her limits. It doesn't mean you totally acquiesce to their moods and let them run your life. It does mean that you plan ahead, prepare for the known roadblocks and land mines, and create an environment where the child (and you) can have a successful outing that doesn't end in frustration, anger and tears.

This is another common reason for the loneliness of raising a handicapped child. Sometimes—actually, a lot of the time—it is easier to just stay home and cocoon in the comfort of an environment that has been carefully groomed to meet your child's needs. Why risk the very strong possibility of having to deal with a public meltdown or even an in-car temper tantrum when you and the child can just relax in your safe place?

I tried this for a while, often saving my necessary trips to Walmart or the office supply store or Lowe's for those times when I knew I would have childcare available. Once my daughter reached her teen years, it became easier, as I could leave her to take care of her brother, which basically meant keeping the door to her room open so she could hear him and make sure he wasn't hurting himself or roaming the house in look of a snack or something to chew on.

That's another thing about the daily life of raising a handicapped child: being completely aware of your child's habits and attractions. Angelman Syndrome kids are obsessed with water. When they see or hear water, they want to be in the middle of it. That could be a kitchen sink, a bathtub, a toilet bowl, a pet's water dish or a yard hose. When I take Danny to a pool, I have to be completely ready to get in the water with him the moment we get there. There is no time to find a suitable lounge seat, spread out towels, put all our stuff down—when he sees the water, he is unstoppable. That's not a problem if I have prepared for that by making a trip in to get everything set up before I take him in. But if I show up at a friend's house for a cookout and they have a pool that I wasn't expecting, even if it's a cool sixty-five degrees and there are still winter leaves floating in the water, I am in for a fight-to-the-death wrestling match with Danny, and will probably be sitting either inside or on the far edge of the crowd away from the pool. Even though his mental capacities are greatly limited, he has an iron-clad memory for things like that, so I will be spending most of the evening redirecting him.

Bottom line: make your life easy and know your surroundings before you enter with your handicapped child. I try never to take Danny to a friend's home, church, park or even doctor's office without first stopping in to survey the environment for possible hazards to his physical health and my emotional well-being.

I tip my hat to those special ed teachers, aides and student assistants who voluntarily venture out into the world at large with their challenged charges. Many of these kids have specific physical triggers that can set them off—loud sounds, bright lights, traffic, automatic doors, car horns, even crying babies—and a trip to the local Walmart is almost a guarantee of some level of disaster for one or more of the students. I secretly tailed them one day to see how Danny responded, and I was blessed beyond measure to see the results. Yes, many of the kids, mine included, did at least one thing that resulted in some sort of intervention by the chaperones, but it was all handled with grace and kindness.

Yes, they encountered some unwelcome stares from other customers, but they also received a lot more smiles and even a few high fives. I don't really know what getting a high five or a pat on the arm from a perfect stranger means to Danny, but I have a pretty good idea that it was a huge blessing and spiritual lift for the stranger. And maybe it was a reminder to some of those frowning customers that they need to have a little more grace in their lives.

My childhood on a dairy farm taught me at an early age that there are inconveniences and frustrations in life that you just have to get past and learn to handle. Cows are dumb animals, and those that are producing milk (on which your family's financial health depends) need attention at least twice a day, no matter what. You can complain about it, resent it, make plans to escape it one day, but that doesn't change the fact that those cows are going to have to be milked early in the morning and late in the afternoon. Every. Single. Day.

Raising a handicapped child offers the same opportunities for frustration and anger. But that's a choice. Every day offers unlimited chances to observe God's grace in our lives and to allow Him to strengthen our feelings of grace and acceptance to those around us, starting with our own highly imperfect child. When you are frantically changing your child's soaked clothes because he wet through his diaper just as the school bus pulled into the driveway; or you have to stop your car on a side street and step out of the vehicle to have an important business conversation because you have to get your kid to the doctor but this call is one you have been waiting on all day and your kid is yelling at the top of his lungs because he wants to go fast; or you find yourself sitting in the church lobby during service again because the music was a bit too much for your kid this particular morning and he was too excited and too loud to stay in for the sermon—you are living large in the handicapped child world.

And you get to choose. To be rightfully frustrated. Or angry. Or envious of those parents with "good" kids. Or to just want to give up and go home and let him go back to watching *SpongeBob* while you relax on the deck with a cool drink and a moment's peace.

But you can also choose to just hang with it. Ride out the big wave of emotion. Keep a positive attitude and focus on helping the child get through this difficult moment. And probably find that the people around you are less condemning and more sympathetic than you expected. After all, chances are that many of them are parents, too, and have all spend time in the purgatory known as the "terrible twos" with their children. It is in these moments you can learn valuable, life-changing lessons about your child, other people and, most importantly, yourself.

Because, ultimately, there is not much you can do to change your child's long-term prognosis. Your child is who he or she is. The question is—what is God's plan for this child, and me, and what do I need to do about that, right now and every day? Just because your child is handicapped and less than "normal" doesn't mean God doesn't have a plan, and that he or she isn't part of it.

Your child is unique. And so are you. You both have special talents, experiences and blessings to share with those around you. How you handle your child's "bad" behavior may just be the greatest blessing some mom or dad will have on that day. It may give them hope to get through a challenge they are facing with their own kids.

Your normal may not look like anyone else's normal, but how you deal with it can be the greatest sermon they may ever see or hear. Don't fear it. Learn from it and take that special light God has given you and let it shine for all the crazy, confused world to see.

People are watching you. I know that as parents of handicapped children it is easy to feel like the whole world is watching—and judging—every inappropriate move your child makes, and every inadequate response you have. We try to shelter our kids from becoming the unwelcome center of attention. We hover around them, watching for wandering arms, grabbing hands, growing stalactites of drool dripping from their chin, and some behaviors that would land "normal" adults in jail for the night.

But the truth is more people are watching you with awe and wonder. They are amazed at your patience, your steadfast attention to your child, your ability to carry on a conversation, keep your child's hands and feet in check, effortlessly maneuver the minefields of Walmart shopping aisles, and do it all with a smile. You want to bring glory to God and reach other people for His joy and hope and peace? This is it. What may look like low-level chaos to you possibly is bringing conviction and even repentance to someone you encounter who is convicted with how blessed they are with the problems they are dealing with every day compared to yours.

This is not something we get prideful about or lord over others. Our kids are who they are, and we can choose to see them as a blessing or a curse. This is our normal. And it is no better, or worse, than everyone else's normal.

Chapter 16
FINDING BALANCE IN AN OFF-CENTER WORLD

"Train up a child in the way he should go; even when he is old he will not depart from it."
— Proverbs 22:6

One Sunday, shortly after my marriage to the nurse had failed and we were all still reeling from the emotional chaos of the previous six months, I took the kids to church and then to McDonald's for lunch and some quality time on their indoor play-area equipment.

As we were leaving, I put Danny in the back seat of the van, buckled him in and went around to the back to stow his wheelchair. I came back around just in time to see Chrissy slamming the side door to the van closed with Danny's hand sticking through the doorway (probably trying to grab Chrissy's hair). My immediate reaction was to yell at Chrissy to STOP!!!!!!!!!! That scared her, which caused her to start crying, which caused Danny to start wailing, which made me think his hand had in fact been crushed by the slamming door.

I yanked the door open and grabbed Danny's arm to inspect the damage, ignoring Chrissy's sobs as she stood next to the van. In typical Danny fashion, as soon as I grabbed his arm, he began whacking on me and laughing, thinking I wanted to play. That allowed me to turn my attention to calming down my now-hysterical daughter.

I assured her I wasn't angry at her and that I had only yelled as a reflex to try to stop something bad from happening. Through her tears, I realized she was saying, "I'm so sorry, I didn't mean to hurt Danny" over and over. And there it was. A chance to affirm her, to thank her for being so caring about her brother, to assure her that we all make mistakes and sometimes people even get hurt because of those mistakes, but that doesn't mean I am angry at her or love her any less.

Then her A.D.D. kicked in and she started talking about a bird that was picking at a discarded hamburger bun just a few feet away. We headed home for just another typical afternoon in the life of my little atypical family.

One of the questions I am often asked about raising a handicapped child is how I made that work with my *normal* child, my daughter Chrissy. In retrospect, the only answer I can come up with is the same I know many of my friends who don't have a handicapped child in the home would give: "Only by the grace of God."

The key is being aware that this normal child has her own unique gifts, challenges, fears and dreams, and just like every other child in the world, wants to be loved, accepted and affirmed. My daughter had a unique set of circumstances to navigate, and having a handicapped brother was just one of those facts. Of greater importance to her was that she was being raised in a broken home by a father struggling to keep his own head above water, she had been moved halfway across the country and put into a new school where she had to make new friends, and was living and playing in the part of the country which offered oppressive summer heat, the possibility of tornadoes and the ever-present reality of fire ants.

She also suffered from A.D.D. and depression. The first was controlled pretty well by medication (after some difficult days as we tried to find the right one and the proper dosage). The second issue was more complicated and never completely resolved.

Ironically, these are probably the two biggest mental health issues her father battles (notice the present tense here; still fighting after all these years).

Fortunately, Angelman Syndrome has no debilitating physical effects, besides poor balance which leads to an inability to walk independently. And Danny loves being outside and around people, so going to Chrissy's sports activities were not a problem (except they were usually on late afternoons when I would come home from work exhausted, or weekends when I was trying to catch up on housework or working at my job).

Danny loved going to Chrissy's baseball and volleyball games. She would practice or play, and Danny and I would sit on the sidelines, often on the ground where Danny could pursue one of his favorite activities, throwing dirt or grass leaves into the air and watching it get all over himself and/or me.

At school, Chrissy found that there were actually some benefits to having a handicapped brother. As I had long been known by many school personnel simply as Danny's dad, Chrissy became known as Danny's sister. Everyone knew Danny, and everyone seemed to have a Danny story, largely because as part of the mainstreaming program required by law, schools now take the special needs kids to classes like band and P.E., where they could "participate," which, for Danny, often meant yelling and banging so loudly that he had to be removed from the room.

When I went through this same school system, I found there was a definite benefit to having had older siblings who had left their marks (both good and bad) on teachers and administrators ahead of me, and it was comforting and heart-warming to see Chrissy benefiting from Danny's trailblazing. In general, the kids at school liked Danny and treated him with respect, and some of those good feelings naturally flowed to Chrissy.

Also, by the grace of God, I was blessed with a daughter who has a good heart and who deeply loved her brother. Because of him, she also developed a love for other handicapped kids, and for the adults who worked with them daily. She even worked in the special needs classes her senior year as an aide and, like me, soon found an appreciation for how easy Danny was to care for, compared with some of the other kids in the class.

But it wasn't all sunshine and lollipops. Danny's needs often interfered with hers. There were times when we were late or just missed her activities because Danny was sick, or exceptionally rebellious and uncooperative, or had appointments of his own that had to be met. Probably the biggest intrusion was with my time. I was often unavailable to deal with Chrissy's crisis du jour because I had to attend to Danny. There were too many times when I would just send Chrissy with her friends and her friends' parents to some event I should have attended; I wasn't there to share too many seemingly insignificant moments that mean so much to a fragile teenager.

Chrissy never complained, and we have a wonderful, honest relationship now. But I know I have some regrets about those days, and

I'm pretty sure she does too. We just choose to focus on today, and not worry too much about the past, except to learn from it.

Bottom line to achieving this balance between your handicapped child and your normal child is making sure that you are honest, open and empathetic with your non-handicapped child. That means sharing your fears and failures with that child (which means having a relationship built on openness) so that she can feel comfortable sharing her own fears, failures and frustration with the cards she has been dealt.

Finding balance in the often off-centered world of raising a handicapped child means being intentional about making time and expending some of your limited energy on each child. There is a daily routine—a normal—to raising your handicapped child and once you find that place, it is way too easy to simply rest there. But that is a breeding ground for neglect and resentment, and before you realize it you have two handicapped children.

As the sixth of seven kids raised on a dairy farm, I had some experience with being an afterthought and being lost in the shuffle of daily duties. If I wanted quality time with my dad, I had to fit into his world, which meant going with him on his daily rounds to the feed store, cattle auctions, equipment repair shops and the field. I cherish those times six decades after the fact.

And as luck with have it—actually, as the perfect, beautiful will of God would have it—my childhood had also provided a unique grid of reference for me to deal with this particular problem many years later in my life. A few years before I was born, my older brother had fallen into a vat of boiling lye water being used to clean our milking machines. He was two years old at the time and suffered third degree burns from his calves all the way up to his shoulder blades.

My parents threw their badly scalded son into their old car and raced the five miles to our little rural hospital, where the doctor stripped all the burnt flesh off, showed my mother how to change the bandages, gave him something for the pain, and sent them home with little expectation that he would survive the next few days.

This was 1949 and there were no burn units in our area at the time. For the next couple of years, our tiny house on a windy North Texas hill became host to a revolving door of grandparents, aunts, uncles, neighbors, church ladies and others who came to help care for and entertain my brother.

By the time I came along three years later, the worst days had passed, the amazing healing had taken on a life of its own without the need for extra outside intervention from friends and family, and a new normal had settled on our household. But the scars on my brother's back, and on my parents' psyche, were permanently set.

During the excruciating hours and days following the accident, my dad blamed himself for not preventing this tragedy, and had promised God that he would do everything he could to make my brother's life good if only he could be healed. I grew up in the long shadow of an older brother who was obviously and undeniably the apple of my father's eye. He was the favorite, and I was next. Then my little brother was born, and he became the center of my mother's world. I was the in-between.

I don't resent or blame either of my parents for this reality. It is what it is. But it left me with scars of my own, yearning for unconditional love, acceptance and appreciation, so I became a people-pleaser, manipulator, liar, relationship addict and eventually an alcoholic as I used it and drugs to ease my pain and give me self-confidence.

Since no one ever sat me down and explained what had happened and why my brother was treated differently, I assumed it was because he was better than me, more deserving of love. I couldn't see anything special about him, so the difference must be in my lack, not his excess.

I didn't even understand all this until I had become a single father, moved back to Texas and attended a ministry training program at the church we were attending. I was fifty years old at the time, and thought I understood my life, but there it was. God had prepared me for raising both my kids through my own experiences as a child. He was making that old mess, and the messes I had created time and time again throughout my life, into a way toward a better path that I could use to bless my children and many others.

It started with being honest with myself, and with my daughter. It meant giving her what I hadn't received—information and attention to understand why things were the way they were (including many of the struggles she saw her dad battling) and space to share her own feelings and needs. There is only one way for that to happen—spending time focused just on her. Speaking openly and honestly to her, and listening intently and without judgment.

As often as possible, I tried to include both my kids in everything I did. Being a single parent often necessitated taking them with me to work activities and the few social outings that sneaked their way onto my busy schedule. We went to church together. We went to Danny's doctor appointments together. We went to Chrissy's school events together. Danny was happy to go anywhere, and Chrissy was more than just a good sport about it.

Years later, when Chrissy had married and was living in her own home, Danny was a part of the life she shared with her husband and her friends. He stayed with them while I worked, and he was just another person hanging out on the sofa in the living room, watching them play video games and doing life together.

I know I was blessed with a sweet and patient daughter, but I still believe the parent sets the tone for the household. I probably should have done more things just with and for my daughter, but for me the key was to make it all about "Team Atkins"—not "Team Danny" but "Team Atkins." And God had to be the team leader.

"Coaching Danny's special needs baseball team gave me the opportunity to share some unique quality time with Danny and get to know many of his handicapped peers."

Chapter 17

PLAY BALL—AND DANCE— AND BLOW BUBBLES

"Weeping may tarry for the night, but joy comes with the morning."
– Psalm 30:5

A sharp wind whistles across the field, stirring up giant clouds of sand and forcing the small band of baseball players to duck their heads and cover their faces. The coldness of the April morning has caused the players to don sweatshirts and jackets, hiding their uniform shirts and making it impossible to know who is on which team.

One player, Teddy, slowly makes his way onto the field, oblivious to the cold and the wind, as he is completely focused on the ground in front of him. He clutches tightly to his walker and moves ever so slowly in fear of tripping over the mild transition from the sodded perimeter of the field to the sandy infield. When he encounters third base, he drops to his knees and crawls over it as one of the "baseball buddies" transfers his walker and helps him get back to his feet. The buddy also carries Teddy's beloved toy microphone, an ever-present prop for his version of reality. Teddy will need the mic to sing "Take Me Out to the Ballgame" and to deliver his ongoing play-by-play of the activities this morning.

In our little town, we call it Special Needs Baseball. It's known as Miracle League in other places. Or Little League Challenger Division. Or Champions' League.

Regardless of the name, the idea is the same: to give people with special needs an opportunity to share in one of the simple joys of childhood—playing a game of baseball with friends. For my handicapped son, but especially for me, it has been a true Godsend.

In the daily loneliness and apartness that comes with raising a special needs child, spending a couple of hours on a Saturday morning with other special needs kids and adults (our youngest player was four years old; the oldest was seventy-three) was a joyful, almost surreal, step back into the world that all the other kids took for granted. The rules are simple: every player gets an opportunity to bat, to field a ball and to throw a ball, regardless of his or her unique physical reality. Truth be told, Danny really didn't care much about the actual baseball part of this, but he loved interacting with his buddies (especially if they happened to be cute high school girls), and sitting in the sand throwing handfuls of it into the air to watch it blow away or simply fall back into his lap.

But for me, and a lot of other parents of handicapped children, these Saturday morning get-togethers were a literal breath of fresh air.

To watch a group of special needs kids and adults celebrate tapping a softball a few feet in front of home plate, or receive a standing ovation and high fives from a line of players and coaches waiting at home plate, or just get a hug from one of the many high school age volunteers, is to feel, even just for a moment, that you are not quite so alone in this strange life you are living.

In fact, the number one topic of discussion I hear when we parents of special needs kids and adults get together at these games and the end-of-season parties is how wonderful it is to just be with others who really, really understand what our daily lives are all about. (A very close second topic is the frustration we all have with some governmental or school agency that is making our lives more difficult than necessary with ridiculous regulations or miles of red tape and bureaucratic BS.)

Parenting is difficult enough for kids who don't have disabilities. Sit in the stands at any youth sporting event and listen to the conversations about stupid school rules, obnoxious coaches, mean girls, bullies, the seventh circle of hell known as the teen years. Everyone has a story, and everyone has understanding and empathy with your plight.

But it's harder to find people who can relate to your ongoing fears about the long-term prognosis for your child's *condition*, or a new governmental regulation that may impact the services you child receives, or just the physical or emotional exhaustion that is starting to overwhelm you and swirl you down into an abyss of self-doubt, depression and resentment.

And once your child "graduates" from high school (in Texas, Danny was able to stay in the school system until he turned twenty-two), the loneliness and apartness can increase exponentially, because your child has nowhere to go during the day and you have lost some of the most valuable and beloved members of your team. Through these special needs sports programs, at least your child has a chance to spend some time with his or her peers, and you have a chance to catch up with many of the people who have been such a big part of your lives for the past sixteen or seventeen years.

The value of this amazingly simple program is beyond measure. It is certainly a far cry from how things were back when I was growing up. The handful of special needs students at my small school were mostly kept out of sight, gathering each morning in the room below the band hall. I never really knew what they did out there. Come to think of it, I guess I never gave them any thought.

In the 1950s and '60s, parents were often counseled to put their special needs children in institutions "where they have people who are trained to take care of them properly." In fact, keeping your mentally handicapped child at home was often considered to be an immoral, selfish act on the part of the parents, because not only could they not "properly" care for that child, but trying to do so would inevitably negatively impact their parenting of their other children.

As part of my freshman psychology class at North Texas State University, I had a chance to tour part of the Denton State School. The experience left me shocked and depressed. But I had no more contact with the special needs community for nearly twenty years, when I reluctantly joined it as a parent.

Thankfully, warehousing the special needs community in state schools has fallen out of favor, and so has much of the stigma and ridicule often aimed at "those people" who looked and acted differently from the rest of us. Keeping people like my son in the public school system and in the public at large has been a great benefit for them, and for society.

In fact, the success of our special needs baseball program and the effect it has had on the young volunteers who help out has led to several other events created and managed wholly by a couple of teenage girls looking for a community service project. My little Texas hometown now hosts a Special Needs Youth Livestock Show where special needs youths have the opportunity to parade an animal such as a hog, sheep, dog or rabbit through an arena with a local television personality as emcee and an enthusiastic crowd cheering them on as cameras record their every move. They each receive a blue ribbon and a photo with a pretty high school girl wearing a sash, but I think their greatest joy is being up close and personal with their "show" animal.

Also, through the baseball program, a group of volunteers have developed a separate activity for those people over the age of fifteen to get together once a month for dances, movies, pool parties, concerts and other activities that give them a chance to learn and practice better social skills, have some fun and give their parents and/or caregivers a night off.

This same small community each summer puts on a weeklong day-camp for special needs. More than 100 "campers" and twice that number of volunteers spend four half-days singing, dancing and playing games.

Though brief interludes in the daily routines, the long-term benefits of these activities on the special needs members of our communities cannot be overstated, because they provide families who so often feel left out and "other" with a chance to relax, enjoy themselves and see their kids cheered and loved. For a few hours, your kid is no different from all the kids on the soccer field across the parking lot. And as a parent, it is encouraging to look around at all the total strangers who are showering your child with high fives, hugs and encouraging words. Maybe the world won't be so bad for them, after all, once you are gone.

Because once you, as a parent and/or caretaker for your special needs child, get past the craziness of doctors' appointments, therapy, school meetings, diaper changes, baths and feeding, late at night when you have a chance to sit with a cold one or a hot cup of coffee and think about the future, you wonder—what will happen when I can't do this any longer?

I have had many well-meaning friends and family pose that question to me, usually couched in careful terms like "have you ever considered putting Danny in a home somewhere so you can have a real life of your own?"

I admit that sometimes I haven't been particularly gracious in my response to their concern. First of all, what exactly is this "real life" of my own to which they refer? I guess they mean one without all the worry and work of caring for a 175-pound adult who functions as a moody eighteen-month-old child. One where I could go out to dinner on a whim, or sleep late on Saturday, or have an adult conversation without being interrupted by impatient banging on the wall because the sippy cup needs refilling.

OK, I get that. But in reality, for me and for most of the caretakers I know of handicapped individuals, this life is not just our truth—it is our true north. I've had several careers and an even greater number of significant others, I've lived all over the country, I've been cursed and praised (often by the same people), I've known fleeting success and devastating failure. None of it amounts to anything significant and lasting.

But raising my kids, especially Danny, has put everything else into perspective. It is the hardest thing I've ever done, and I can't imagine not doing it. Even during the three weeks a year when he visits his mom and I am free to come and go as I please, within days I find myself missing not only him but the routine. I have no purpose. I am back to just being.

God, in His wisdom, took a lonely farm kid who spent his youth riding a 1940s-era Farmall tractor around a twenty-acre field dreaming of someday doing something great and meaningful but without any particular talents or skills, and gave him the task of raising a child who would never speak but would touch everyone he met deeply just with his big smile and happy demeanor.

It's a simple life. It can be really boring sometimes, and some days I get the yearning to jump in my truck and head out on the road with no destination in mind other than "somewhere else." But Danny keeps me centered. He is my gift, my anchor, my purpose.

If you have a handicapped child, you probably know exactly what I mean. If you don't but you know someone who does, be patient with them. Call them occasionally and let them do all the talking. Put an arm around them when you see them and let them know they aren't all alone in this strange world they call "life."

After years of searching for the answer to the big questions of why and what next, chances are they have found the answers are in the questions themselves. It's hard for them to explain to outsiders—all you "normal" folks. But that's OK. We won't hold it against you. Besides, it's time to fix dinner and start getting ready for bedtime.

Chapter 18
DOCTORS AND HOSPITALS

"For he has not despised or scorned the suffering of the afflicted one; he has not hidden his face from him but has listened to his cry for help."

– Psalm 22:24

I n 2009, the H1N1 virus (aka swine flu) swept the land, leaving more than 200,000 fatalities in its wake. The media deemed it an "epidemic," although it was nothing compared to the 1916- 17 version that killed more than fifty million worldwide, but that was before the 24-7 news cycle and social media. The twenty-first century version resulted in closed schools, cancelled public events, and led to a short-term panic run on pharmacies and doctors' offices in search of a flu shot.

Since Danny's time with the Ketogenic diet, his seizure activity had been limited to only those times when his body was struggling to fend off some other illness such as strep throat or one of the three-day bugs that regularly ran through his special education class at school. Sometimes he would show significant signs of illness and I could up the dosage of his seizure meds to ward off the coming storm.

Occasionally, I was caught completely by surprise. One very cold night when he was twelve, I awoke with a start about 2:00 a.m. sensing something wasn't right. I checked on Chrissy and she was sleeping soundly among her giant pile of stuffed animals. When I went into Danny's room, I found him lying on his back completely rigid, with arms stuck straight out to each side of his trembling body, and he was making that terrible gurgling and smacking sound that always came with the seizures.

My immediate reaction was to get him off his back so that he did not aspirate the vomit which I knew from experience would be coming soon and profusely. The problem was that with his arms locked in position, I couldn't just roll him over. Even though I was still considerably larger than Danny, when he locked up like this, moving his arms down required Herculean strength. It was easier to stand him up, spin him around and put him back on the bed face down.

I had learned to measure episodes like this with three criteria: frequency, intensity and duration. I began to take close notes of his facial expressions and the tremors, trying to determine how often the seizures were coming, how long they were lasting and how strong they were.

Once I saw that we were getting relatively short bursts of seizure activity (less than a minute each) at a rate of more than three every five minutes, I knew it was time to call the doctor. Within a few short minutes (although it seemed like an eternity at the time), she called me back and told me to continue monitoring what was going on, and if this continued for another fifteen minutes, to give him a dose of the antiseizure medication I carried in his bag at all times.

By this time, Danny was pretty much totally unresponsive to my pleadings, going from working his mouth hard and his eyes darting back and forth wildly during the seizure, and just lying there completely out of it when they passed. I watched and waited, trying to remember exactly how to administer the medication, something I hadn't done in years.

Fifteen minutes passed and the seizures continued so it was time to act. Now where was that bag? Oh yeah, it was still in the van. When I stepped out of the house to the carport I was hit by just how cold it was and a light sleet stung my face. I grabbed the bag out of the back seat, rushed back in and frantically pulled the applicator out of its package. Danny was in one of his "in-between" phases and was just lying there lifeless. I couldn't be sure if he was sleeping or had slipped into a catatonic state.

I read the instructions, inserted the end of the applicator into Danny and pushed the medicine steadily into him. Danny's reaction was immediate and dramatic, which makes sense since I was injecting a near-frozen liquid into his warm body. At first, I thought it was another seizure coming on, but when I took two seconds to think about what I was doing to him, I felt really dumb and bad for him.

Still, the medication worked, and he soon responded appropriately when I spoke to him and tickled him. Another hospital trip averted.

By the time of the swine flu epidemic, Danny had grown significantly (he was now seventeen years old and a stout 175 pounds). The school had been hit hard and attendance was down sharply. The special needs kids are always at a high risk because their ability to fight off illness is often compromised by their physical or neurological issues, and they are usually unable to accurately express their health concerns. With non-communicative kids, you have to know what normal looks like so you can catch the nuanced changes early.

With Danny, it started late one evening (these crises always seem to happen when the world is sleeping). Danny started throwing up the little bit of food I had gotten him to eat. Once that was gone, he threw up some really foul-smelling bile. Then came the blood—red at first, then brown (they call this coffee grounds).

Throughout all this, which had transpired over nearly two hours, Danny and I had engaged in a wrestling match that would have pleased WWE fans. I was trying to keep him from getting on his back, where he could aspirate his vomit. Danny had other ideas, and a whole lot of determination to win this battle.

Finally, exhaustion calmed him down long enough for me to park his sister on top of him so I could dial 911. We could hear the sirens from miles away, an eerie sound on our quiet street. I gave the EMTs a quick overview of our situation, along with a brief tutorial on Angelman Syndrome, which seemed silly, as we were only a four-minute ride from the hospital. But it is something parents of special needs kids get used to. I don't know whether it is the health care workers' genuine interest in this rare condition or just a standard CYA procedure, but they always want to know exactly what it is, what it affects, what the prognosis is and what they need to be watching for.

Vomiting up coffee grounds was something we had encountered frequently. Once, during a doctor's visit, he started throwing up, which went quickly from food to bile to red blood to coffee grounds. An ambulance was called and he was transported to a children's hospital forty-five minutes away. He threw up the entire way, and when he got there they still pumped a significant amount of old blood out of his stomach.

This bloody vomit issue is a perfect example of how a simple health problem can lead to a true medical crisis. Danny didn't know how to care for his nose by simply blowing it. Consequently, he would swallow whatever post-nasal drip he experienced, and would scratch the inside of his nose to a bloody mess when he picked at it. He swallowed the blood, which pooled up in his stomach until it became toxic and led to the unstoppable vomiting. This all lowered his seizure threshold, and the breakthrough seizures just confused everything and everyone trying to fight the battle on his behalf.

Let me just say here that this is my experience as a parent. I am not a doctor, and there may be health care professionals out there who would read that previous paragraph and call BS on that. I've encountered that attitude by E.R. staff and other medical professionals, and I can't say for a fact that they are totally incorrect.

But as a parent with twenty-five-plus years of caring for a handicapped person, and as someone who has a high regard for logic and process, all I can say for sure is I know what I have seen and heard in exam rooms. And without a doubt, the best doctors are those who actually listen to the parents and defer to their judgment when there is no clear, definitive answer otherwise.

It was during our E.R. visit with this swine flu episode that I heard the words I think all parents of special needs kids long to hear during their child's medical emergencies. The attending physician called Danny's doctor to update her on what was going on once Danny was unloaded from the ambulance and safely settled into his temporary home in the exam room. At the end of the call, the doctor turned to the nurse in charge of his care and reported, "She said to do whatever his dad wants done because he knows what he is talking about."

As usual, up to this point they had been arguing against giving him any anti-seizure medication, thinking the gagging and the vomiting were just more flu symptoms. Danny was miserable, going from dry heaving with occasional bursts of "coffee grounds" oozing from his mouth, to slipping back into an almost catatonic, non-responsive state.

By now, this had been going on for nearly three hours and we were both totally exhausted. Still the dry heaves continued, and they wrenched me as much as they did him.

Finally, they administered the anti-seizure medication and the change was immediate and dramatic. Danny calmed, was responsive to the nurses and to me, despite being barely able to stay awake. He slipped into a peaceful sleep and we were transported to a private room, where we would spend the next three days quarantined, since it turned out we both were suffering from the swine flu.

The point of this story is that, once again, I, the parent and resident expert on Danny, knew in my gut and in my heart, what was going on. Not the medical professionals with all their training, equipment and textbooks. As the parent, never allow yourself (and your kid) to be intimidated and/or bullied by someone who has a bunch of letters after their name. You are the expert. That doesn't mean you never listen to reason and good advice. It just means remaining true to what you know you know you know.

There is a reason God chose *you* to be this person's caretaker. Don't be afraid to walk the walk *and* talk the talk.

Chapter 19
THE ROAD FINALLY TAKEN

"Come now, you who say this, 'Today or tomorrow, we will go into such and such a town and spend a year there and trade and make a profit—yet you do not know what tomorrow will bring. What is your life? For you are a mist that appears for a little time and then vanishes.'"

— James 4:13-14

A few days after my sixty-fifth birthday, I met with my financial planner to discuss how best to protect the meager savings I had cobbled together and begin making real plans for the day when someone else would be spending my money.

After asking me how long much longer I planned to work ("as long as I physically can," wasn't an answer he could plug into his computerized questionnaire, so we agreed on ten years for discussion purposes), he asked, and I quote, "When do you plan to die?"

The fragility and temporary aspect of our lives is something I think most of us think about from time to time, even at an early age, but I don't think I have ever been so arrogant as to put a number on when I "plan" to die. It's not something I feel is really in my power to set a date to or plug into my calendar.

And yet, as a parent of a special needs child or adult who will, hopefully, outlive you by many years and require at least the same level of care you have been providing all these years, you **must** have a Plan B. In my case, I hope that we can stick with Plan A for at least another fifteen years (which would take me to eighty years old, at which point I will probably be needing some of the same cleaning and feeding services I am now giving to Danny).

But I am a realist. I could have a heart attack or stroke (both are part of my family medical history) at any time, which would limit greatly my ability to lift, dress, change or walk Danny to the car. I could be in an accident. I could develop cancer or see a rapid deterioration in my mental functions (both of which are also in my immediate family's medical past).

Regardless of how old your child is, how old you are, how much family support you have surrounding you or what your financial condition is, the reality is that you should start making some long-term plans as soon as possible and start setting those wheels into motion immediately.

When I came back to Texas as a newly single parent in 2001, I visited the local mental health mental retardation office to see what services were available and to get Danny (and Chrissy) enrolled in the state's medical insurance program for kids that was offered at that time.

They presented an alphabet soup of acronym-named options we could select from (like CHIP, HCS, MDCP, CLASS). I dutifully signed up for the ones that seemed most immediate at the time and took home the information to review regarding the others.

Unfortunately, I let other issues of the day that seemed more urgent take precedence, like finding our own place to live and someone to care for my kids when they weren't in school. These long-term plans slipped to the back of my very cluttered desk. Several years passed before I got around to taking a hard look at these papers, and by then several thousand other applicants had stepped in the waiting list lines ahead of Danny.

As I write this, Danny, who just turned twenty-seven years old, has been on the CLASS waiting list in Texas for more than ten years, and the best guess is that it would be at least seven or eight more years before his name was called and we could begin receiving services from that program, which would be a huge part of Plan B once I am gone. That means nearly twenty years of waiting to know what his long-term future would be.

Navigating the waters of federal and state programs for the disabled can be confusing and frustrating, because the language describing the programs and their requirements was obviously written by attorneys who, in their attempts to cover all the potential bases and possibilities, have made it nearly impossible for a neophyte to understand any of it and make informed choices. There are people who specialize in these and can be hired to guide you through the process. I found the best sources to be those who have already made the journey on behalf of family members and/or patients (therapists are great sources for this, as they have a good idea of what services are offered by the different programs).

The key to making good choices is to have an open mind, a firm grasp of reality (both of your kid's long-term prognosis and your own health and well-being), and a team of professionals around you whose judgments and advice you can trust (this would include doctors, therapists, school teachers, aides and counselors).

My best source of information and encouragement turned out to be a lady at Danny's school who was on Danny's ARD team (in Texas, there are counselors and teachers assigned to special needs students who meet with parents annually to go over the school's plan for addressing the student's needs. That is called an ARD—for Admission, Review and Dismissal. In Georgia, we had an IEP team, which dealt with his Individual Education Plan.) The counselor on Danny's ARD team had a mentally handicapped brother and because of her training was the primary decision-maker for his care. She not only pointed me in the right direction to look for services, she put a firm boot in my rear end to start making things happen. I had already wasted about seven years, and neither Danny nor I were getting any younger.

Probably the biggest, and hardest, decision you will face when looking at these programs is who you want to provide care for your child once you can no longer do that. In the old days, kids like Danny ended up in an institution, like the state school I had visited in Denton during my college days. I remembered some of the higher functioning young adults I encountered living in small apartments and achieving a small amount of independence in their highly controlled environment. They cooked for themselves, cleaned, took care of their own dressing and personal care needs, and even kept a "work" schedule of sorts, going to the sheltered workshop on campus to practice the productive skills they were being taught by therapists.

But I also remembered the wards of the more highly involved—hydrocephalics in their helmets sitting on chairs next to their beds, a young boy beating his helmeted head slowly against the wall and mumbling incoherently, hyperactive boys wrestling with caretakers who were trying to redirect them into whatever activity they were attempting to perform.

In the last thirty years of the twentieth century, these institutions fell out of favor due to some highly public reports of rampant abuse and neglect inside their walls. The buildings were shuttered or repurposed as out-patient service centers, and their residents were moved into smaller group homes, returned to their families or, in too many cases, simply put out on the street with a monthly check and a "guardian" to manage their money and their care.

So, Danny's long-term care options would seem to be one of two simple choices: either a group home or a personal care assistant with whom he would live full-time once I have reached the end of my ability to provide those services.

My plan was to work as long as possible but start drawing full Social Security benefits when I turned sixty-six. That would allow me to sock away as much money as possible while we waited for Danny's name to reach the top of one of the waiting lists for his long-term care options. Depending on which one he qualified for first, he would either go into a residential care home or his sister would be responsible for finding someone to provide daily care out of her home.

The problem with making long-term plans is that life has a habit of not going as we planned. A few months before my sixty-sixth birthday, the physical strain and emotional stress of my job, coupled with the daily responsibilities of caring for Danny, finally pushed me to the breaking point. I could not continue the chosen path without suffering possible severe consequences. My father had started having mild heart attacks and strokes when he was in his late fifties, and here I was almost ten years older than he was when that started.

Plus, several of my friends were fighting for their lives (and in some cases, losing the fight) against cancer. I was scared and mind-numbingly exhausted. Something had to change, quickly and drastically. My greatest fear was that I would have a debilitating stroke, leaving my daughter with hard choices to make not only about Danny's care, but mine as well.

At least, the short-term financial future didn't look all that bleak. I was blessed with an understanding boss, who accepted my decision to take a step back from my job responsibilities yet continue working. The money I gave up for my new job description was compensated for by the Social Security check I would begin receiving shortly after my sixty-sixth birthday.

When I applied for my retirement benefits, the helpful government worker on the phone gave me a very important piece of advice. Knowing that I was caring for a handicapped child, he warned me to be ready for some land mines along the way, as Danny's monthly income would now be tied to my benefits, and sometimes the left hand of the government doesn't know or understand what the right hand is doing. (More on this in the next chapter.)

The job change certainly took a lot of pressure off my day to day life, and I was able to actually get a full night's sleep on a regular basis. Financially, we were doing well, moving toward the day when I would be debt free and even less worried about the future.

But there was still the unresolved issue of Plan B. Who would take care of Danny when I couldn't do so any longer? The financial planner's question lingered in the back of my mind—when would I die? More importantly, when would I reach the point where I would be unable to do what I had been doing for most of Danny's life?

Of course, I obsessed on this for months. I worried about it. I talked to everyone who would listen. I became depressed and despondent. No one seemed to have a good answer.

But God...

One day while I was out making my rounds at work, my son-in-law called. He was a Navy nuclear technician working on an aircraft carrier being rebuilt in Newport News, Virginia. He and my daughter had been doing some long-term planning, considering what they would do when his contract with the Navy expired in a couple of years. That brought up questions about where they would live, should they continue to rent or invest in a home, and how having kids would impact those decisions. Just hearing that made my heart race; you always want to see your kids looking past tomorrow.

"We just wanted you to know that anytime you decide you want to move out here and have some help with Danny, you are welcome," he said. And there it was. The answer. Not AN answer. THE answer. I once had a pastor tell me that you know it's God speaking because what is being said is something you would never say. This was beyond just a Plan B. This was affirmation that I didn't have to worry about this (or anything else for that matter). God's got this, just as He always had, even when I was too blind to see it.

Within weeks, the wheels were turning quickly toward a major life change for all of us. A perfect home in a perfect neighborhood popped up on my daughter's real estate app and the financing went amazingly smoothly. Danny and I made it to our new Virginia home just in time to see the cherry blossoms turn yards, sidewalks and streets into pink pathways.

Whatever the future holds for Danny, and me, would be in the context of a whole family unit. I wouldn't have to face it alone. I would be able to not only secure Danny's future, but weave my daughter, her husband and any children they might have along the way into this amazing tapestry God has been building ever since a blustery spring morning in 1992.

Life isn't easy, with or without a handicapped child. But it is possible. And beautifully messy. When you look back and see God's direction and correction along your winding, sometimes bumpy, road, you realize that nothing has happened just by chance. Going all the way back to my brother's accident three years before I was born, through my life on a dairy farm, through the many mistakes and bad choices I had made through my adult life, through my divorce from the kids' mom—all of it played a significant and vital role in my life, and the lives of my children.

Chapter 20

GOVERNMENT PROGRAMS
AND OTHER MADNESS

"Blessed is the one who finds wisdom, and the one who gets understanding."

– Proverbs 3:13

Even though God had provided a way ahead for Danny and me, there were still a thousand details to work out. At the top of the list was making sure the services he was receiving through Medicaid would continue once we moved from Texas to Virginia.

Because even though Medicaid is a federally funded program, it is administered by the states. Each state has different qualification criteria, different program names and different agency names. As much as I love my birth state of Texas, the truth is it is really not all that good for people with disabilities and their caregivers. Since the state doesn't have an income tax, it relies completely on property taxes and sales taxes, both of which are subject to fluctuations in the economy (especially the oil and gas industry).

In addition to learning some basics of genetics, neurology, nutrition, physical therapy, seizure medications and treatment, special needs education laws and how to properly insert a suppository, having a special needs child means acquiring some basic knowledge of their legal and financial needs and rights. Knowing the ABCs of MDCP, SSI, CLASS and HCS will have major, life-long implications for both you and your child.

Whatever program you choose, chances are there is a waiting list of applicants for it. Some of those lists have literally thousands of names on them. In Texas, we were on a couple of waiting lists for more than ten years.

I am a fairly educated person with a journalism background, so I know how to research and ask the right questions. And yet, we sat waiting while many of Danny's peers were already receiving those program services because I totally misunderstood how the system works.

Once Danny turned eighteen, he legally became an adult and everything changed, including the type of services he received and how they were funded. At first, it was great. For three years, I was paid to care for him in the evenings and on weekends (most of his days were spent at school, so he needed no paid care then. I paid for after-school care out of the money the state paid me.) That income was a true Godsend, as my daughter was heading off to college and I needed more money than ever to buy her a decent car and pay for her tuition and rent. Plus, her departure cost me my free live-in baby-sitter who could watch Danny while I ran errands or worked.

Danny did age out of the Medically Dependent Children's Program (MDCP), but at least the state doesn't just kick the handicapped and their families to the curb. We were moved to a similar, scaled-down version of MDCP which would serve us until he came off the waiting list for CLASS. Every year, a nurse would come to my house to requalify me for that program, and we went through the same questionnaire that was submitted and reviewed by a bureaucrat in Austin. As always, bad is good, so any hospitalizations or seizure events were actually good to have. I admit there were times when, in the middle of the night and Danny was having one of his coffee-ground vomiting episodes, I picked up the phone and dialed 911. I probably could have handled it on my own, but the value of having a hospital stay on the record when it came to re-certifying him for the program was invaluable.

And so it goes in the world of handicapped daily life.

When Danny turned twenty-two, everything changed again. He aged out of the school system, which meant he needed paid care during the day while I was at work. At the same time, the rules for who could be a paid caregiver changed. Any relative living at the same residence as he did could not receive payment for his care. A significant portion of my income was stripped away and I had to find someone else to take care of him during the day.

Then, shortly after Danny's twenty-sixth birthday, something happened with the state's management of the Medicaid program, and they made a drastic reduction in the number of hours of care they would fund. For several years I had received funding for forty-plus hours a week of personal assistance and protective service care. In addition, I got sixty hours a month for respite care, which was designed to give me as the primary caregiver a break and a chance to take vacations or deal with other family crises, such as funerals.

But because Danny's seizure issues had become less and less of an issue and he had no other medical problems, the state decided this level of care was too great. In my final year of living in Texas, I was caught up in a months-long battle over cuts the state wanted to make because he did not qualify for skilled nursing care (something we had never asked for or received). They reduced his weekly care hours from forty-three to twenty-nine. I had to make other arrangements or pay out of pocket for care he received while I was at work (and I usually worked forty-five or more hours a week). Also, since he did not qualify for skilled nursing care, he no longer qualified for respite care, which meant no more extended time off for vacation or family emergencies.

I appealed and was granted a full hearing with a state arbitrator. The phone hearing involved a half dozen interested parties (five representing the state; me representing my son). It was official, formal, cordial and the arbitrator seemed genuinely concerned about my issues. A few weeks later I received the official ruling that although she was sympathetic to my cause and understood my frustration, the rules were the rules and she had no choice but to uphold the state's position.

Once again, as we in the handicapped world learn early on and come to accept after months and years of frustration and tears, it is what it is. You just have to face the reality and move on.

The other significant legal change you will face as your handicapped child ages is that once he or she turns eighteen, that person is an adult with certain inalienable rights that don't automatically flow to the parents. You will have to go to court and be named his or her guardian. Even though it is really a simple procedure (assuming you are not involved in some custody battle and have been providing that care for years), you will have to hire a lawyer and go to court.

You will also have to pay for your child's attorney, known as a guardian ad litem, whose job it is to represent the interests of the child and help the judge determine who is best fit to be the child's legal caretaker. You may also be required to put up a bond to guarantee the court that you are serious about this responsibility, and each year you will have to file a certified report with the court on how you are managing his or her health and well-being.

This may seem like a lot of government interference, but as a newspaper reporter I had the unfortunate experience of covering several stories where grown men, mostly veterans, were having to go to court to have guardians removed. The care the guardians provided was usually nonexistent. They got the person's monthly Social Security or disability checks, gave little or no money to the person, and didn't care that the person for whom the money was intended might be living on the street or literally starving to death.

The other legal issue you need to address for the special needs person in your life is how their affairs will be dealt with when you pass. When you determine your child has a lifelong disability, go see an attorney and have a trust set up in his or her name. When your child reaches adulthood, long-term benefits are based on the person's income and assets, and if you die without a proper will and trust set up, inheritance can have a dramatic, costly effect on those benefits.

Remember, when it comes to legal and financial issues for your child, bad is good, worse is better. The key to all these programs is getting your child qualified for Medicaid, because that is where the health care benefits come from, and other services use the Medicaid requirements to determine their eligibility.

And just because your child is admitted to the Medicaid program, don't assume your challenge is over. This is why you need a trust for your child, so that when you die, anything your handicapped child would inherit from you will go into that trust instead of directly to him or her. Any asset (property, savings account, stocks, bonds, etc.) can and will be used to determine the financial need and can have a direct impact on the amount of benefits your child receives. Sometimes grandparents mess things up by leaving a sizeable gift to their handicapped grandchild for long-term care, but don't realize that their gift can cause more harm than good.

This is why you need a will and a trust, which means you need a good lawyer who understands financial planning. That's going to cost some money, but it is money well spent.

As a parent of a handicapped child, it is easy to feel isolated and alone, especially as a single parent. But you are never alone. With the internet, you can quickly locate resources, support and an understanding ear who will help you walk this often-hard road. Never be afraid to ask for help. Never be so prideful to think you have to have all the answers and must solve all the problems on your own.

Take that from someone who tried. And failed. Thanks be to God, though, I finally learned the lesson.

Chapter 21

NAVIGATING RETIREMENT BENEFITS

"Therefore take up the whole armor of God, that you may be able to withstand the evil day, and having done all, to stand firm."
– Ephesians 6:13

When I decided to start taking full retirement benefits at the age of sixty-six, I set off a string of unintended consequences that took months of written communication and lengthy phone calls to resolve. Here's how it works. When your child is admitted to the Medicaid program, that also qualifies him or her for disability income (Supplemental Security Income). There is a maximum amount the government will pay each month; in Danny's case, about $750.

When the parent starts drawing Social Security, the handicapped child's check will be based either on the previously approved disability amount, or one-half of the monthly amount being received by the parent, whichever is higher. There is no choice in the matter. You must take the higher amount.

In our case, half of my monthly Social Security check was greater than what Danny was getting, so he got a raise. But since he no longer qualified for SSI, that meant he no longer qualified for Medicaid. Except he did qualify. It's just that many in the left hand of the federal government didn't know what the right hand had approved.

Fortunately, when I was applying for my Social Security benefits, the government worker warned me that this might happen and to be prepared to fight for it. "Congress has passed a law specifically for people like your son," he said in that life-saving phone call. "Don't let anyone tell you differently. They will probably try to cancel his Medicaid."

Which is exactly what they did. Within weeks of receiving my first monthly Social Security check, Danny got a letter informing him of his impending monthly financial bonus, which was followed by another government letter saying that because he was no longer receiving SSI, he could no longer receive Medicaid benefits.

This was a huge, and scary, turn of events. Medicaid pays for all of Danny's doctor's visits (which really amount to only one or two a year, but who knows when that might change), hospital stays (also infrequent, but each one runs into the tens of thousands of dollars), his diapers and, most importantly, the daily care he received from an attendant, which allowed me to work full time.

At least the government is prepared for the objections. In the letter, there was a phone number I could contact—a number which was soon programmed into speed dial on my cellphone. The first worker I spoke to said I had heard wrong, that there is no law allowing the children of retired parents the opportunity to receive Medicaid once their SSI has been cancelled. It only took about twenty minutes of arguing for us to agree to disagree, and I moved on.

I called the Social Security Administration back—the agency that had warned me that this might happen—and a very friendly and helpful worker assured me that I had not heard wrong. There is a law, and she emailed a copy of it to me.

Armed with that, I called the number off Danny's letter again, and this time was connected (after another forty-minute round of arguing and frustration on both ends of the phone) with a supervisor who knew exactly what I was talking about and agreed to personally rectify this error.

Before any benefits were lost, the problem was resolved, and we were able to move on to the next crisis.

And this is where it gets really confusing. I think I am correct in my assessment of what happened next, but I'm not completely sure. Either way this IS an accurate account of the highly stressful season of conflict I faced in the months leading up to my decision to move out of Texas (a state I dearly love, except for a few parts that I really hate).

Medicaid is a federally funded program that is managed by the states. That's why benefits can vary so much from state to state. For example, I learned that Texas is one of only three states that does not provide dental care for adults with disabilities. Dental care is a big deal for Danny, because you can't just take him to the local dentist for routine checkups and simple procedures. He is not going to just sit there and say "ah" while somebody sticks assorted tools and needles in his mouth.

When Danny was seventeen, his case manager with the company contracted by the state to oversee his care scheduled a dentist appointment. I took him to a dentist office and we succeeded in wrestling him into the exam room chair. But he would do nothing but grit his teeth and grin at the dentist, no matter how much she cajoled and tried to trick him. She scheduled an appointment at a children's hospital in Dallas. An anesthesiologist sedated him, he was whisked away for extensive X-rays, the dentist checked the X-rays and conferred with the oral surgeon who was there, then proceeded to pull and/or fill all of his problem teeth.

It was a very efficient, effective and I am quite sure, expensive, trip. And it was the last of the state financed dental care he could receive in Texas.

A few weeks after I resolved the problem with his Medicaid eligibility, Danny received another letter from the state saying that in a review of his records, they had determined that he did not qualify for Medicaid benefits because they had determined he was not really handicapped. I was caught between stunned disbelief and uncontrollable rage.

This time, I had a state agency number to call, as they were the ones who made this amazing decision. Again, the first person I encountered was totally unhelpful. She said that either something had changed about Danny in the past few months OR perhaps I had made an error with some paperwork I had submitted. I knew both those suppositions to be impossible, as there had been no change in Danny's abilities, and I had filed no paperwork. "Well," she offered, "probably the best thing for you to do is to just refile all your paperwork and then we can get this right."

If you have ever filed paperwork for any government program, such as a student loan, home mortgage or disaster assistance, you know that we aren't talking about going online for ten minutes and filling in the blanks. You have to provide lots of "proof" documents, which in Danny's case meant gathering records from assorted doctors, therapists, schools, banks and whoever else the government deemed relevant to the decision-making process.

This was a process that was guaranteed to take months, and I only had a few weeks before the termination would take place and the benefits would go away. There is an appeals process where you can buy some time, but the whole thing was so ridiculously insane, I decided to go another route.

"Who else can I talk to, right now?" I demanded.

I was transferred up to the office of the public ombudsman, which was tasked to deal with unsolvable problems and unhappy clients. Once again, this higher level paid off immediately. "They always do that," the extremely helpful lady offered. "I will go in and fix that right now." With a few clicks, it was all done, all good. "Is there anything else I can do for you?" she asked.

I was stunned, and a bit overwhelmed (and not completely sure I trusted this quick fix). "That's it?" I asked.

"Yep, you'll get a confirmation letter in a few days about this conversation."

"Oh, okay then. Great. Thanks."

But the state wasn't quite done messing with my blood pressure just yet. I headed out to Virginia for a Christmas visit with my daughter and to check out the possibilities of relocating there in the spring. It was a great, exciting trip, and I returned home on New Year's Eve to find a letter from the state awaiting me. "Ah, my confirmation. That lady was really telling the truth."

And there it was. At the bottom of a page full of disclaimers and explanations and "what to do if you don't agree with this decision" information, was a simple statement in all caps: "BENEFITS DENIED. TERMINATION DATE JANUARY 1, 2019."

I cannot adequately express my shock and rage. And here it was the eve of a national holiday, which meant I couldn't even call and scream at someone for TWO DAYS. At least, at that moment I was able to immediately and completely put aside any and all lingering doubts I had about the decision to leave my beloved home state and spend my remaining days on earth in some other ZIP code far, far away from this madness.

By the time 9:00 a.m. rolled around on January 2, I had cycled through many, many rounds of brilliant arguments, threats, tear-inducing pleas and general rants in my head, so I was prepared, and exhausted, when another very cheery person in the state ombudsman office answered my call.

She looked up her copy of the letter I had received, reviewed it and asked what was the problem. "What is the problem? WHAT IS THE PROBLEM? I'm losing all my benefits for my son, which means I can't get any day care benefits, which means I'm going to have to quit my job to take care of him myself, which means I am going to have to let the sweet lady who watches him for me go, which means both of us are probably going to have to file for bankruptcy—what do you mean WHAT'S THE PROBLEM?"

Her calmness was beyond frustrating. My life was falling apart, and she was saying to just take a breath and give her a chance to fix this. I had heard (and believed) those words before. I was not amused.

"Let me put you on hold for a minute," she said. By the time she came back, I had decided rage obviously wasn't going to work, so perhaps begging would be a better approach.

"Mr. Atkins, according to this letter, your benefits are fine. No change is recommended."

As I stared at the letter, I wondered when I had crossed over into the Twilight Zone. "Do you see the box at the bottom of the page?" I asked, numbly. "Can you read what it says? I just want to make sure that you and I are looking at the same letter."

"It says benefits denied."

"And what does that mean to you, exactly?"

"Well, it means you can't receive the benefits you requested."

"So how is it that my benefits are fine and that no change is recommended if they have been denied?"

"Well, I see how that could be confusing. But you have to keep reading on the back. You see where the box says Benefit Effective Date and underneath that it says ongoing. Well that means your benefits are still in force and there is no start or end date, they are just ongoing."

My head was really hurting and I was seriously considering reverting to my lifelong habit of drinking too much, even though I hadn't touched a drop in 5-1/2 years. "Then why does it say benefits are denied and were terminated as of yesterday?"

"Oh, that's probably something that was put into a previous letter and should have been deleted from this one. It's just a data entry oversight. So you see, it's all good. Is there anything else I can help you with today?"

And there it was. Just as I had encountered so many times over this quarter-century-plus journey, I stood face to face with the complete disconnect between what the world was saying and what I was seeing. Her statement made no logical sense. I was to just ignore what the letter said, in black and white lettering on official government stationery, and trust her word. My financial future hinged on it, as did the financial well-being of my caregiver. My job and my mental health hung in the balance as well.

Trust her.

No, trust God. God who had been with me at every confusing, scary step along this journey. Having done all, I simply put my trust in Him, thanked the lady for her help, and let it go. There was nothing else I could do anyway. Just trust God, and move on.

To God be the glory: the benefits continued. And I began making plans to leave Texas once and for all.

"A few weeks after his 27th birthday, Danny and I moved in with his sister and her husband in Newport News, Virginia. This move brought Danny within miles of two of his favorite activities: playing in the ocean and in the beach sand."

Chapter 22
LOOKING BACK;
LOOKING FORWARD

"Count it all joy, my brothers, when you meet trials of various kinds, for you know that the testing of your faith produces steadfastness. And let steadfastness have its full effect, that you may be perfect and complete, lacking in nothing."

– James 1:2-4

anny is laying on his Futon bed, licking his fingers and staring out the front windows, or at the wall, or at his guardian angel whom I can't see, or just into space. Who really knows? He seems content. He has been quietly doing this since he woke up an hour or so ago, giving me a chance to sit on the patio just outside the glass door to our basement living area in our new home in Virginia.

It is a glorious spring morning, full of soft breezes, bright blue sky, chirping birds and the incessant hum of multiple leaf blowers cleaning my neighbors' driveways and sidewalks. It is just three weeks after Danny's twenty-seventh birthday, and the move is complete and has been blessedly non-eventful. We have found a place where Danny can have plenty of fresh air, room to roam about in relative safety, neighborhood wildlife and beautiful flowers to marvel at, and enough family around to keep him protected and entertained.

He recently received his new Medicaid card, so now we are just waiting to hear from the insurance company that handles that for the Commonwealth of Virginia so we can determine exactly what services will be available for him. That will also help finalize his daily schedule which will, in turn, allow me to figure out what kind of employment I will be able to pursue. For now, though, we wait.

Thanks to the money he and I receive from the government each month, and the attention I gave to getting out of debt these past few years, we have the luxury of waiting in peace. And in that peace, I have found the opportunity to look back and review all the challenges, and blessings, that I was too busy to notice these past few years.

I remember being at one of my daughter's softball games some fourteen years ago. It was a beautiful evening, and Danny and I sat in the dirt near the end of the dugout for Chrissy's team, close enough where I could watch her play yet far enough away from the rest of the crowd where Danny could engage in one of his favorite activities— taking handfuls of dirt and throwing them a few inches into the air (usually just far enough to cover his legs in dirt).

And of course, I had my large cup of iced Diet Coke, laced with several shots of vodka, at my side. This was the perfect family portrait of my highly imperfect family at the time. Dysfunctional but highly functioning family bliss.

As the game drew to an end and I began gathering up all of Danny's stuff and cleaning the dirt off his pants and legs, a lady came up and stood right in front of us, looking down at us with a strange smile. I prepared for either a lecture about letting Danny get so dirty, or the inevitable interrogation about Danny's condition.

"I just wanted to tell you," said started (oh no, here comes the lecture), "that you are amazing. You are doing it right, and that all of us parents see it. Thank you and bless you."

I honestly did not understand what she was talking about, partly because I was distracted by Danny trying to grab my large drink mug that contained the real truth about who I really was at that time.

"I'm sorry," I stammered. "What did I do?"

"You have been sitting on the ground for the past hour giving your full attention to your son. You never picked up your phone or read a book or got up and wandered off for a minute. You obviously are totally focused on your son, but you have just let him be who he is and do what he wants to do. That is really sweet, and amazing. It made all our evenings."

I could only mutter a quiet "thank you," not knowing how to respond to such a huge compliment and also not wanting her to see the shame and red-faced embarrassment such words of praise always brought me. For one, whatever I did was just me coping with tonight's reality as best I knew how in the easiest way possible. Chrissy had a ballgame I needed to attend, and Danny has a tendency to get bored and fussy when he's stuck in some unfamiliar place, which means I have to be always prepared to deal with his outbursts at any given moment.

And my coping mechanism for all this at the time was to numb my boredom and stress with alcohol. Sitting alone in the dirt with Danny kept me from others who might get within sniffing distance of my drink cup.

But the lesson was clear. As a parent, you are constantly being watched by the world, including your children. You are constantly teaching them about life and how to deal with it, whether you like it or not. When it comes to parenting, actions definitely speak way louder than words. Telling a lie is one thing, although sometimes it's hard to remember what lie you have told to whom. Living a lie is much harder, because you have these unguarded moments and the truth slips out. Those moments tend to happen when you are with the people you are most comfortable with—like your children.

As the parent of a handicapped child, you are always on stage when you are in public. Little kids and rude adults will stare. More responsible adults will either smile and say hi, or avert their eyes and ignore you, but will often be caught casting furtive glances as you and your child wander the shopping aisles or stand in line at the check-out. You usually don't notice these, though, because you are totally focused on keeping your child from grabbing items off the shelf or the arm of some innocent passerby.

We are unique. Or, more bluntly, we are weird. Odd. Not ordinary. Different. *Special*. People notice and many are touched in some way. Just accept it. Deal with it. In fact, embrace it, because in our weirdness, we have the opportunity to touch others in a unique way, and possibly make a huge difference in their mundane lives.

I do not consider myself a particularly honorable person. In fact, for most of my life, I have felt more shame than honor. That tends to be a recurring theme among drunks and liars when they take a painful, honest look at their lives.

But I can't tell you how many times I have had friends, acquaintances and even strangers comment that they are so touched by how I have committed my life to caring for my handicapped son. They are *honored* to even know me.

One particular *honor* outbreak occurred as I sat in the lobby of my church on Father's Day about six years ago. Danny was perched in his usual spot on a sofa just inside the front door. As soon as those entering received their church bulletin from the greeter, they were met with Danny's big grin. Most would stop and say hi. A few brave ones patted him on the back of the head or grabbed his waving hand. And several, too many for my comfort, would look at me and say, "Happy Father's Day. God bless you."

One lady made her way across to room to do all three, adding "you are the best dad I have ever known."

Little did they know the pain all those kind words inflicted on me. Actually, there was a lot they didn't know. They didn't know that I had spent the previous evening sitting in Danny's room, throwing down one stiff vodka and Coke after another while he watched one of his Disney movies. They didn't know that my head was throbbing from another hangover headache. They didn't know that I felt like the lowest form of vermin alive. And they certainly had no idea that Satan had me right where he wanted me. He was OK that I was in church because he knew that he could really beat me down with shame, guilt and unworthiness as long as I was so close to God's presence and God's people.

But God…

But God had another plan that morning—a plan that would change me forever and would benefit both my children greatly. That very morning, amid all my shame and guilt, God put a new friend in my life. Patrick was bringing a Christ-centered 12-step recovery program known as Celebrate Recovery to our church. He became my sponsor and accountability partner. His encouragement, and that program, led me directly to sobriety and a new relationship with God, and gave me a new family made up of a lot of other struggling souls in my community. I have not had a drink in more than six years, and everyone around me has benefited from that great blessing.

God loved me in spite of my failures—not because there was anything special or honorable or admirable about me. He loved me because I am His child—his highly imperfect, limited, often foolish and frustrating child. I get that, because that's how I feel about Danny.

For more than a quarter of a century, I had tried to be the best parent I knew how to be—nothing more, nothing less. I had no experience or preparation for raising a handicapped human, except my experience of caring for a bunch of cows who had to be fed and milked twice a day regardless of what was going on in the world that day.

I had to find my way in a world where there are often no clear paths, no easy answers, no guaranteed results. I had to rely on my gut instincts, intellect, trusted family and friends—and God.

At the end of the day, each day, it has always been the "and God" part that got me through. I certainly didn't get it all right, and there were many, many doubts and fears and fits and starts and feelings of abject failure.

But God…

That's why I wanted to write this book. That's what I want readers to take away from it. This isn't a story about a great dad—this is a story about a completely broken dad in the hands of a great and good God.

If you are walking this path, or know someone who is, take heart. The Lord is with you. We are the ones with the honor of caring for "the least of these," and God has promised to never forsake or forget those lesser-thans—or the people who walk with them.

Life is hard, even for the normal people living normal lives. It is not something you want to try alone. I have so many people to thank for being God-with-lips along the way. I couldn't have done it without my late brother Doug, my pastor-mentor-encourager Elaine or my longest-serving friend Sandra. I couldn't do it without all my brothers and sisters in Celebrate Recovery.

I certainly could not have done this without my amazing, sweet, loving and kind daughter Chrissy and her equally sweet and kind husband, Brody, who have welcomed Danny and me into their home and will someday take the Danny-care mantel on themselves.

Yes, you are different, and you are special, but you are just like the rest of us. And it has nothing to do with your handicapped child. Because he or she is also different, and special, and just like the rest of us. We are all children of a merciful and loving God. We are all able to do *anything*—with His help. We are also able to do *nothing*—apart from Him.

God has a plan for you—and your child. I know it's hard to see when you are changing a messy diaper at 3:00 in the morning or sitting next to your poor baby in another ER exam room with all manner of machines beeping and pumping around you. It's easy to forget how blessed and loved you are when you collapse in your recliner at the end of a long, exhausting day.

But God…

Hang in there. Believe. Cry. Make an effort to laugh and dance. Live.

God bless you.

ACKNOWLEDGMENTS

If it takes a village, as the saying goes, to raise a child, it takes a small city when it comes to raising and caring for a special needs child who requires constant care and attention for a lifetime. Even when it seems like you and your child are on a long, lonely, unfamiliar road to nowhere, when you look back you see that you were surrounded by many "angels among us" every step of the way. In addition to family and old friends, there are doctors, therapists, teachers, aides, school administrators, case managers, ministers and prayer partners.

So when it comes to acknowledgements for this book, the problem is knowing where to start and the fear is of leaving someone out. There have been so many people who have crossed our paths over these past 27 years, who blessed us with their wisdom, insight, connections, directions, questions, answers and just a smile or hug at the exact time when it was needed most.

Some key players aren't around to see this story in print, starting with my dear, sweet parents who taught me about being responsible, working hard and never giving up no matter what. A special thanks to my dad who passed along his love of and gift for storytelling. And there is my oldest brother, Doug, who was in the right place at the right time when my marriage fell apart and I returned to Texas broken in every way possible—financially, emotionally and spiritually. He babysat my kids while I worked and he babysat me through some of the deepest, darkest struggles in the early days of single parenthood.

As God drew me back into His presence and His plans for my life, He blessed me with an amazing church home, Crossroads Church in Decatur, Texas. The founders, elders, pastors and staff at that wonderful place not only accepted me, they encouraged, challenged and taught me about serving others, and through that service I found the meaning of God's love for all His children. Thanks to my dear friends Barry Garrett and Darren Embree for their never-ending support and love and encouragement.

I've really struggled to find the right words of thanks for another pastor on that staff, Elaine Huff. She was the children's pastor when I first found my way there. Through her friendship and leadership (including some swift kicks to my backside and arm twisting when needed), I found a whole new way to get out of my problems, fears, self-pity and low self-esteem issues through serving. She tricked me into teaching in kid ministry (something I ended up doing for nearly 10 years), she put up with my endless questions about how to raise my daughter through her tweens and teens, and she taught me how to believe in myself and trust God's plan when I just wanted to sit on my deck and feel sorry for myself.

Along the way, I was also blessed with amazing and patient employers, who always encouraged me to keep my kids first and gave me the grace to do that when crises arose. Ronnie and Janet Hess were true gifts from God when I returned to Texas with no money, no job, no place of my own to live. They took a chance on me even though I had no direct experience in their industry, and their support for me and my family never wavered for more than 13 years.

Joey and Cerissa Gardner not only supported my family commitments, they also encouraged me to draw closer to God and rely on His provision and direction every day, even as the work world often challenged us to our core. Their love and devotion for their own children and for God inspired me and was the perfect place for me to labor as I moved through the final years in the workforce. Much of this book was written while I was working there, and the time spent with Joey discussing God and His desire to be a part of all of our lives had a huge impact on helping me see God's ever-present role in my struggles.

In 2013, when I was really struggling with alcohol abuse and depression, a ministry came to our church that would completely change my life. Celebrate Recovery is an international ministry to help people deal with the hurts, habits and hang-ups in their lives. It is a 12-step program, but it goes far beyond the issues covered by Alcoholics Anonymous and Narcotics Anonymous, and is driven by the belief that our "higher power" is none other than Jesus Christ. From the moment I attended my first meeting, I put aside a lifelong drinking habit.

Again, there are too many who have impacted me deeply through this amazing program to try to name names (plus there is that whole confidentiality thing to consider), but I do want to thank my sponsor, Patrick Thomas, and his wife, Jillian, who walked with me through my early days of sobriety, as well as teaching me and encouraging me to be a leader in this awesome program. To all my brothers and sisters in CR at Crossroads Church in Decatur, and now at the CR group I help lead at Calvary Chapel Church in Newport News, Virginia, thank you for your unconditional love and acceptance, not only of me but of Danny, who has been a part of (and sometimes major distraction for) many meetings and small group sessions.

I honestly don't think I would be here today if not for the people God has put in my life through Celebrate Recovery.

And then there are the people who knew me long before I became a parent, who seem to have always been a part of my life, through all the good and the bad.

My longest-serving friend, Sandra Coale, graciously and patiently helped bear my burdens, usually over the phone late at night when my daily chores were done, the kids were in bed, and I had time to give a little attention to my own pain and depression.

Carol Cates opened her heart and home to my little, dysfunctional family at a time when I was at a crossroads and needed direction. Her love and support were guardrails for my heart and my often cloudy decision-making habits.

This book would not have been possible, in many, many ways, without the contribution of Patricia Conley. Not only is she the mother of Danny and Chrissy, she was the primary caregiver during those early, difficult, scary days when we were still trying to figure out what Danny's issues were and how best to deal with them. She filled in many blanks for me as I wrote this book, correcting my fuzzy memories of what happened when and why, and in providing insight into how certain options were chosen. Additionally, her excellent copy-editing skills help make this book more readable and grammatically inoffensive.

We serve a God of details and no coincidences. As I was looking for someone to review my manuscript, a conversation with some of the people in my CR group led me to the husband of Kim Spano. Kim, it turns out, is a longtime employee of Morgan James Publishing. Kim put me in touch with David Hancock, the company's founder and chief executive officer.

Thanks to David Hancock, Founder of Morgan James Publishing as well as Jim Howard, Publishing Director and Margo Toulouse, Author Relations Manager, for making the process of moving my book from manuscript to final product an exciting, fun, not so scary and always encouraging journey.

This book would never have been possible without my amazing daughter, Chrissy, and her equally amazing husband Brody. Chrissy has brightened my life and blessed me beyond description as I have watched her grow from precocious kid to a beautiful, confident young woman. She and Brody recently opened their home and their lives where Danny and I have found a loving place to find rest, peace and security as we head toward the day when I won't be able to physically care for him anymore.

Finally, my greatest and deepest thanks are to my God and creator, and to His son Jesus, who died so that we might have hope. For many years, I tried to run from God; I didn't want to hear about all the things I was doing wrong and be judged for my failures.

But God…

He never gave up on me. He was gracious and patient and always faithful to answer my prayers—not always exactly how and when I wanted them answered, but in reviewing my past for this book I now see that I was never alone. He had this all the time. I just wouldn't let it go. Praise be to the God of second chances. And third chances---and 5,000th chances.

Through my son's silence, and in spite of my many wanderings and failures, God has been faithful. There have been struggles, disappointments, worries, setbacks, sleepless nights and desperation. But God gave me the strength to never give up on my family because He never gave up on me.

Praise be to God.

ABOUT THE AUTHOR

Being raised on a small dairy farm in North Texas gave **Ken Atkins** a solid grounding in being responsible for the daily care of cows and crops—lessons that would pay off 30 years later as he struggled to raise his handicapped son as a single parent. His experience as a schoolteacher, newspaper and magazine writer, editor, and in sales provided the skills and experience necessary to write and share his story of love and redemption in *The Silent Son*.

Lightning Source UK Ltd.
Milton Keynes UK
UKHW011830050221
378222UK00011B/314

9 781631 950643